TRAINING THE MODERN SHOW JUMPER

*My special thanks to my father
who turned my eyes toward horses,
to my mother
who taught me to look further out,
to my brother for his support,
to all great riders and horsemen
who have written down their experiences;
to my wife Christiane and my children
for their patience and consideration
and to all
who in an irreplaceable act of friendship
test-read this book*

Elmar Pollmann-Schweckhorst

Training the
Modern
Show Jumper

Elmar Pollmann-Schweckhorst

Translated by
Sigrid Eicher

KENILWORTH PRESS

First Published in Great Britain in 2006 by
Kenilworth Press
Addington, Buckingham
MK18 2JR

Published in the USA in 2005 by
Trafalgar Square Publishing
North Pomfret, Vermont 05053

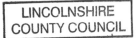
Originally published in the German language as *Springpferde-Ausbildung heute* by FNverlag, Warendorf, 2002

Disclaimer of Liability
The author and publisher shall have neither liability nor responsibility to any person or entity with respect to any loss or damage caused or alleged to be caused directly or indirectly by the information contained in this book. While the book is as accurate as the author can make it, there may be errors, omissions, and inaccuracies.

British Library Cataloguing in Publication Data
A catalogue record for this book is available from the British library.

ISBN 1-872119-93-X

Printed in China by Midas Printing International

Book design by mf-graphics, Marianne Fietzeck, Gütersloh
Cover design by Heather Mansfield

Cover photo: Alois Pollmann-Schweckhorst riding Aperio.
Illustrations: pp. 36, 41, 44, 47, 48, 57, 61, 62, 66 ,67, 70, 71, 80, 82, 83, 94, 100, 103 (2), 134, 139 (5) S. Weiler, Gladbach; pp. 15, 151 Thorwaldsen, steel engraving; pp. 25, 26 courtesy of Bernd Eylers, *Ausgewählte Hengste Deutschlands 1994/1995* (Selected stallions of Germany) [*Die Beurteilung des Pferdes* (Evaluation of the horse), Werner Schockemöhle pp. 439—445]; p. 95 courtesy of Kosmos Verlag: Jasper Nissen, *Parcours- und Hindernisbau* (Show jumping and building obstacles); pp. 125 (2), 126, 130—1: courtesy of *Aachen — Weltfest des Pferdesports 1898-1998* (Aachen world festival of equestrian sports);
Photographs: p. 12 Kleinholz; p. 18 (3) Bild-Report Wagner, Grünstadt; p. 18 (2) Profoto-Team, Delmenhorst; p. 18 Hans-Jürgen Rick, Hannover; pp. 18 (2), 19 (2), 44, 47, 51 (2), 67, 71, 76, 81, 93, 99, 120, 121 (2), 133 MaWe-Bilderdienst, Brohl-Luetzing; pp. 18, 34, 46, 65, 72 (2), 73 (2), 74, 76, 79, 81, 84 (4), 85 (4), 86, 92 (2), 93, 101, 104 (2), 105 (3), 115, 128, 136, 158; p. 19 Susanne Dufner, Ulm; pp. 19, 22, 23 (2), 24 (2) Werner Ernst, Ganderkesee; p. 28 Foto Mitschke, Hohenstein;p. 31 Franck Papelard, Frankreich; p. 55 Norbert Schamper, Münster; p. 70 Koctukoba; pp. 75, 104, 111 pro cheval, Walldorf; p. 78 photec—Michael Schröder, Oftersheim; p. 98 Fotografie C.B., Kiel; p. 103 Maximilian Schreiner, Unterstall; p. 118 from *Reiter und Fahrer Magazin* (Rider and driver magazine), volume 5, September/October, 1957; p. 124 Werner Menzendorf from *Die Bilder der Deutschen Reitschule* (Images of the German riding school), Dietbert Arnold, Pferdesportverlag Rolf Ehlers, Bremen; page 127 (top) from *Reiter und Fahrer Magazin*, volume 1, January/February, 1962; page 127 (bottom) from *Reiter und Fahrer Magazin*, volume 3, May/June, 1962; p. 135 from *Farbatlas Huf* (Colored hoof atlas), Christopher Pollitt, Schlütersche, Hannover.

Advisors: Christoph Hess, Director of the FN Training Department; Michael Putz, Erlangen, former Director of the Westfalian Riding and Driving School at Münster, Germany (1986-2000); Isabelle von Neumann-Cosel, Edingen-Neckarhausen, author and editor of equestrian books

"The popular belief that theory is out of place in the art of riding will not keep me from maintaining that there is no perfect art of riding without theory… However, I admit that theory and practice should never be separated as in our art, the body plays an important part."

FRANÇOIS ROBICHON DE LA GUÉRINIÈRE
(1688–1751)

Foreword

Whenever we give seminars and clinics for jumper riders, it always strikes us that "dressage for jumpers" is very often confused with classical dressage. For all its wealth of theoretical details, this book has been written with practical application in mind, is supported by numerous practical examples, and is recommended for practical use. Here, the priorities and goals essential in the training of jumpers are dealt with for the first time. Useful solutions for everyday training problems are provided, and in addition, present day developments are critically scrutinized and problematic subjects are dealt with in an open manner. We think it right and important to discuss problems using actual examples instead of hoping that they will not be spoken of at all. It is made clear that the right way of training for each individual horse must be found, and for this reason, even touchy subjects should not immediately be judged or condemned, but considered and weighed carefully.

In accordance with the ideas of this book, we offer the following advice: be flexible and imaginative and on the lookout for the path your horse will tell you to take. Always listen to what the horse is telling you, as this is the only way to make horse and rider an outstanding team!

Markus Beerbaum
and Meredith Michaels-Beerbaum

Foreword

Elmar Pollmann-Schweckhorst comes from a well-known family with a long tradition in riding and horse breeding. He was a successful show jumping competitor up to the most difficult level ("S," in Germany) and awarded the ultimate distinction by the German National Equestrian Federation (FN), the "Golden Badge" for ten top placings at this level.

The author has written his book on the training of jumpers from practice, for practice. He examines the theoretical connections in the training of horses and riders without losing the practical context. In this, he benefits from his own education and passing his exams for professional horsemastership. And, his knowledge is enhanced by his personal experience and viewpoints. This book offers a wealth of advice for the patient, methodical, and successful training of jumpers, with special regard to the aspects of health and ethics. The less experienced rider will find lots of useful hints to include in his daily work, as well.

Enjoy this book. You will be impressed by the ideas laid out for you. May your everyday work and handling of your horses lead to the harmony based on mutual trust—a trust that can only be developed by long-term training—that should be everybody's main aim. This book can help you achieve your goals.

Christoph Hess
Head of the Department of Education
Section Sport – the German FN

Systems of Training

The purpose of this book is to present the state of training jumpers today and to integrate the various existing methods into a system of universal value. In the case of jumping, the claim that there is a suitable system for all obviously meets with certain problems. First of all, there is the genetic component: no horse is like any other horse (at least, up to now). Second, a rule that may apply to one horse may be totally unsuitable for another; it may be too much for one, too little for another, and then just right for a third.

In addition, human heterogeneity is equally differentiated. Every human being (including riders!) is unique with regard to his or her hereditary abilities, as well as to the environmental influences that have shaped—and continue shaping—him or her. Depending on character, temperament, and environment, one rider will concentrate on areas that are considered totally unimportant or negligible by another. Because of this variety, many seemingly contrary concepts of the right way of training jumpers have developed.

Different Roots

If you compare the training systems in use in different countries and on different continents, you will notice discrepancies in the approaches. Differing concepts are not only due to the knowledge of the people in question, but also due to the different types of horses. English show jumping, for example, has its roots in fox hunting, a fact which is unmistakably reflected in the English way of riding, and occasionally, in the type of their horses.

The tradition of fox hunting was taken by the English to America, but has there undergone a separate development. The importance given to hunter classes hints at the common origin, but for decades, American hunters and jumpers were recruited from the Thoroughbred breed. Consequently, the main emphasis of American riding was to calm and relax high-strung horses. On the European continent, however, the breeding of jumpers first drew on the "utility" breeds: a type that required thorough gymnastic exercising, even sensitizing, and a calculated "tensing-up" in order to make them jump successfully.

Remembering this time, Alwin Schockemöhle told a German newspaper,

Some time ago, everybody wanted to copy the Americans with their blood horses and their riding style, which was adjusted to their mounts. But it did not work with our horses.

The Hannoveraner, 2/74, April, 2002

Today, the type of the jumper becomes more and more the same throughout the world, not least because European breeders increased the percentage of Thoroughbred blood in their horses and because more and more of these were exported to other countries. As George Morris said, "North American riders never understood or preferred the art of dressage until the Warmblood horse forced them to,"[1] which shows how the techniques of training jumpers are assimilating, more and more.

Recent History

The term "classical art of riding" is used much too often, even if the paths shown by the old masters have proven valid up to the present time. In dressage, the basic movements and ideas were established hundreds, even thousands of years ago and have preserved their power and importance until today. This is not the case for the school of jumping, as this form of competitive riding is less than 150 years old.[2] In the twentieth century, modern society's interest in performance, as well as the commercial exploitation of the sport by trade and industry, created a fertile ground for the development of the "show jumping circus" into a peak performance sport. This, in turn, led to the enormous push that jumping experienced in the last few years. Despite all the risks that commercialization may involve, who knows when a social system will again offer favorable conditions for the development of the sport?

There is no doubt that thousands of years ago horses were made to jump small obstacles, but this has nothing to do with the fact that essential elements of jumping were discovered as late as the middle of the nineteenth century. The first "quantum leap" came with the discovery of the forward seat of the rider, which was intended to allow a natural flow of movement and balance. In 1842, this forward position had already been practiced by Kegel, and from 1887 to 1889, by Lieutenant Freiherr von Fuchs-Nordhoff at the Cavalry School of Hannover.[3] Its eventual worldwide popularity, however, was due to the Italian Federico Caprilli, an officer at the Cavalry Schools of Pinerolo and Tor di Quinto.

Today, Caprilli is mistakenly called the inventor of the modern jumping style. This is wrong for two reasons:

1. The forward position in jumping had been discovered and practiced by others. Caprilli's merits were that he transferred the balanced position into a military schooling system and thus essentially contributed to its becoming well known. In its most important characteristic, the balanced seat over obstacles, is still practiced.

2. The forward position of the rider enabled the horse to jump undisturbed. The term "modern jumping style," however, has to be understood in a more complex manner and should be considered as the sum of the processes of development and perfection, which continue up through today. With regard to position and influence of the rider when approaching an obstacle, Caprilli's ideas should be regarded as old-fashioned. For example, the rider's control of the takeoff point and the horse's suppleness did not play any role within the Italian schooling system.

Not every outstanding rider represented a new stage of development. There were

---

[1] Morris, George H., *The American Jumping Style*, New York: Doubleday, 1993.
[2] Ammann, Max E., *Geschichte des Pferdesports* (The history of the sport horse), Verlag C. J. Bucher GmbH, 1976/84.
[3] v. Poseck, "Reitsport im alten und jetzigen Heere" from *Das Deutsche Reiterbuch* (The German rider book), Berlin, 1940.

always riders whose style could not be generalized—either because they were ahead of their time, had found special access to their horses via unorthodox means, or particularly enjoyed experimentation. The methods of some of the riders or schooling centers were especially representative of the concepts and ideas of their time, and "put their mark" on their time. And, by their example, they had considerable influence on the concepts of training jumpers. Guided by such outstanding riders and impressive institutions, I will give a short survey of the development of the training of jumpers in Germany.

The Cavalry School of Hannover

Between 1928 and 1939, a riding style was developed by the instructors and riders of the Cavalry School of Hannover, which became known throughout the world as the "German jumping style." To quote Michaela Otte, author of *Geschichte des Reitens* (The history of riding):

> *For one thing, this style excelled because of its uniformity, for another because it took over the Italian forward seat but did not neglect schooling in dressage. Proceeding from suppleness, rhythm, contact, impulsion, and responsiveness to the aids, the jumping ability of the hindquarters could thus be developed.*

Aloys Pollmann-Schweckhorst, Senior (riding his mare Friedchen) belonged to the generation that was trained by former members of the Cavalry School of Hannover. Characteristic features of his style were suppling the horse with dressage, a forward seat, and established rhythm—but as yet, no control over the point of takeoff.

My father Aloys Pollmann-Schweckhorst was strongly influenced in his riding by the ideas of the Cavalry School. Since childhood he had worked with horses on his parents' farm on the Lower Rhine because during the First World War—and after—all transport and agricultural work was done with horsepower. It soon became evident that he was good at handling difficult horses, and thus he worked a lot with horses and thoroughly enjoyed it. From a very young age, he was passionately fond of riding. At lunch break he used to mount his mare Friedchen[4] and jump over self-made fences. One day, two ex-members of the Cavalry School, Jochen Epping and Hubertus Bischoff, performed at a local show, where out of a sequence of obstacles, they developed a jump-off. After the show, my father measured the distances

▶

[4] Werheid, Hans, *Sport wird bei uns großgeschrieben*, Heider: Bergisch-Gladbach, 1998.

between the fences and copied the sequence at home for training purposes. As it happened, Major Epping came to visit the farm, and the fences caught his attention.

"Who did this?" was his first question.

"Me," my father answered.

"That's incredible, that's advanced level!" he exclaimed.

From that day on, Major Epping trained my father on a regular basis. It was a very successful collaboration, and riding Friedchen, my father eventually defeated elite German riders in one of the then rare advanced competitions offering a lot of prize money.

My father taught me and my brother the basic concepts of the Hannoverian jumping school: suppling the horse through dressage, allowing free carriage of the head and neck, simple bitting, maintaining a rhythmical and fluent canter throughout the course, and acquiring the horse's cooperation in "seeing" a stride.

Controlling the Point of Takeoff

In the second half of the twentieth century when civilian riders replaced the military officers, jumping style became strongly individual.[5] Riders were looking for their own ways and in a certain sense pioneered jumping's development. Each decade had its own models and idols. In the fifties and sixties, Fritz Thiedemann and Hans-Günter Winkler introduced the concept of controlling takeoff. Alwin Schockemöhle can also be linked to this style of riding. The canter strides in front of and between obstacles were divided up more and more deliberately. Less and less was left to the horse in terms of seeing a dis-

tance; the point of takeoff was determined by the rider. Precision was increased in this way, but at the expense of rhythm and supple, unobtrusive influence by the rider—features that until then had been characteristic of the German jumping style.

Control and Rhythm

Alwin Schockemöhle's students, however, represented a new generation. One of them was Gerd Wiltfang, who in the 1970s, heralded a new era in riding. His subtle influence on the horse (which he adapted to the individuality of his respective mounts) was combined with a lightness and rhythm.

I remember watching the finals of the World Championships in Aachen, Germany with my brother Alois. The four finalists—Eddy Macken, Johan Heins (also an ex-Schockemöhle student), Michael Matz, and Gerd Wiltfang—all impressively represented this new way of riding: sensitive, harmonious, rhythmical, and inconspicuously controlling the point of takeoff, thus making the horses jump in a very precise manner. The winner was Gerd Wiltfang, and we (my brother and I) were very inspired. This was how we wanted to ride—just once! (In the 1980s, I actually became an apprentice at Wiltfang's barn.)

Until the mid-eighties, Wiltfang was a top rider with innumerable successes. His clever riding, in combination with his gift for letting horses jump in the most natural way is unsurpassed even today. But, as he relied entirely on his genius and ignored dressage work—despite courses becoming more and more technically challenging—he soon lost his dominating position (to the barn of Paul Schockemöhle, among others).

---

[5] Otte, Michaela, *Geschichte des Reitens* (The history of riding), Warendorf: FN-Verlag, 1994.

In the eighties and nineties, the German jumping style was also influenced by the very successful American and English riders and their natural and light style. Horses were not ridden "with their noses touching their chests"; the times of dictatorial control had passed once and for all. A new generation of young riders was now able to direct their horses in front of and between fences with an—until then—unseen combination of precision and lightness.

Training Centers

At their respective times, institutions such as courtly riding academies; the cavalry schools of Hannover, Pinerolo, Tor di Quinto; the US training center at Gladstone; and Paul Schockemöhle's barn in Mühlen, Germany were known as centers of research and development for the school of jumping. They were a forum for the most talented riders who, mounted on excellent horses, were allowed to dedicate themselves exclusively to perfecting their abilities.

My brother was lucky to be a member of the Schockemöhle barn when it was in the prime of its importance. At that time, the German team for championships almost exclusively consisted of members of the Schockemöhle barn. The riders did not have to pursue any occupation other than the improvement and refinement of their riding. Each was expected to have a broad understanding of equestrianism, but that notwithstanding, there were specialists in all fields. From the blacksmith's workshop to the equine hospital, from the stable manager to the feeding expert, everything was under one roof—even the time-consuming searches for sponsors and talented young jumpers.

Top riders such as Otto Becker, Evelyn Blaton, Ludger Beerbaum, Franke Sloothaak (to whom my brother owes the most, beside Paul Schockemöhle and Manfred "Manni" Kötter) exchanged advice and gave support. And, they learned from each other through observation. For example, if one rider had problems with a specific horse, the horse was ridden by another—and still another—until the suitable rider was found. Of course, there was a lot of competitive pressure, but they considered themselves a team. International competitions were the tough touchstones for this school.

What Does "Classical School" Mean?

What does this well-worn term really mean? Everything that is old and obsolete? Very little of what has been thought and written in the past on the subject of riding horses endures. Whether we read of the martial curb bits as described by Löhneysen in his *Della Cavalleria* (Of the cavalry), 1609, of Baucher's philosophy of "loosening the lower jaw," or of the unnatural movements created by Fillis, they all supported partly misleading concepts. On the other hand, they also discovered and recorded truths. Everything changes, and not everything that was considered "classical" a hundred years ago is seen in the same way today.

Today, when we videos of dressage riders like Otto Lörke, for example, who by their prowess marked a whole century, we feel a slight disappointment in certain aspects. The self-carriage of Lörke's horses is phenomenal, but they show a considerable lack of straightness. All these riders, however, have contributed mosaic pieces to a picture, which even from our present point of view is right and true. Wilhelm Müseler, author of *Riding Logic* and *Equitation: La Formation du Cavalier—Le Dressage du Cheval,* an essential work on learning to ride and school explains, "The classical art of riding may be defined as the method of schooling a horse that, in a natural way, and taking into account the horse's psyche, strives for perfect harmony between horse and rider."

But, this is not all. On the basis of the old experiences, new ones have been gathered, and thus modern schooling theories are enriched considerably. Which new ideas will eventually be termed "classical" depends on their significance to all disciplines and all times.

Tab. XVII.

▲ *A steel engraving after the famous frieze of the ancient Greek Parthenon temple (on the Acropolis). If a person reaching across time and space desired to give a short and apt explanation of the standard of equitation in ancient times, what could be more beautiful and more convincing than this ancient motif? The close-sitting rider influences his horse mainly by weight and leg aids. In combination with a light rein, his stallion develops maximum carrying ability over his hindquarters, which are swung well under his body. The seemingly faraway look of the young rider is meaningful: he seems to give his aids out of experience and practice and without emotion—they are like reflexes from the subconscious mind, and more importantly, from a mind that is perfectly at ease. Horse and rider are one, much the same as a musician may regard his instrument as part of his own body. After more than 2000 years, all these are still distinguishing features of the true art of riding.*

Assessing the Jumper

Anyone who is fond of jumping needs a partner: a horse. When looking for such a comrade, a rider has to ask himself (not only out of economic, but also ethical reasons) whether the horse will be physically and mentally able to handle the related tasks and strains. The assessment of the jumper, therefore, is the first step toward a long and successful partnership.

In general, the younger the horse, the lower the sum of money to be invested. If a larger sum is paid, the greater the uncertainty: it is hope that is bought. In the case of a green horse there remains only—besides the assessment of conformation and motion—a look at the pedigree in order to get an idea of potential. After all, it is due to selective breeding that show jumping was able to develop to the level actually seen in top events.

Assessing the Pedigree

It helps to be able to assess a pedigree when looking for a suitable young jumper. The most important quality that the prospect's direct ancestors will hope to pass on is a high standard of performance. Unfortunately, numerous offspring and at least eight to ten years at stud are needed to evaluate the value of a certain sire or broodmare.

Many breeds and certain geographical areas known for breeding, have produced talented jumpers: France, Belgium, the Netherlands, and Ireland are, beside Germany, considered the main producers of jumpers in the world. But, not only the European Warmblood breeds succeed. In the past, American Thoroughbreds and French Anglo-Arabians have supplied first-class jumpers. The French Warmblood was developed with a focus on jumping—with great success.

Top jumpers may result from the most unusual crossings. Brilliant jumpers such as Jappeloupe de Luze, Galoubet, and Halla were partly of trotter origin, whereas Milton and Marion Mould's small mount Stroller had some Connemara blood. Draft horse blood is found in the lineage of some Irish mares, and when Westfalian breeders began to reorientate their breed from carriage horses to riding horses, the change was based to some degree on draft breeds.

© José Arturo-Chávez-L.

▲ *Thaloc, French Team World Champion 2002 ridden by R. Argot, is a result of breeding for performance. His father, Quidan de Revel, won the team bronze medal in Barcelona in 1992 and was fourth individually. His mother, Lonipierre (Loripierre), was French Championesse at the age of seven.*

A few decades ago there was even a Hanoverian mare called Goldpuppe by Gotthard out of a draft mare, and she won advanced level show jumping competitions. Of course, while jumpers are to be found in many breeds, there is also no breed exempt from sometimes producing untalented individuals, as well.

There are particular areas that do produce gifted jumpers at a higher percentage than others. Thus it is no surprise that, in the last few decades, despite its relatively small stock of broodmares (approximately 8,000) Holstein, Germany, has been one of the top producers of jumpers in the world. It is the only German breeding region that in its statutes has laid down "jumper" as its breeding objective. Jumping ability has been deeply rooted for a long time, as is proven by one of the leading members of the Cavalry School of Hannover:

It should be interesting to know which area produces the majority of good jumpers, and it will come as a surprise that the area—which until a few years ago exclusively produced carriage horses—now supplies the highest percentage of talented jumpers. This occurs despite the fact that Holsteiner horses with their crested necks, high-stepping trot, and round and rolling canter do not really correspond to the picture of the riding horse we may have in mind. Evidence of this is the high percentage of Holsteiner horses among the top jumpers of the Cavalry School.

MAJOR VON BUSSE, 1940

When a breed is focused on a single discipline of riding, it is achieved in less time than when the aim is the breeding of horses suitable for all things: dressage, jumping, eventing, carriage driving, and leisure purposes. This is apparently the reason why most of the German breeding areas try to improve the jumping abilities of their stock by introducing Holsteiner blood. Because there are so few Holsteiner breeders, it was easy to keep track of the lineage of their broodmares, which were numbered and always given great importance.

Broodmare Lineage

"If I want to thank somebody for my successes as a breeder," an old Holstein horseman once said, "I have to go to the graveyard." How the lineage of a broodmare proves the surety of its inheritance is demonstrated by one of the most successful broodmare lines: the Holsteiner line 890—the branch of the mare Bizarre. In the mid 1930s, this line had already been famous for its jumping ability. At that time, German military officers used to buy three-year-old horses, school them for another year, and then send those with the best jumping abilities to the Cavalry School of Hannover. Three-year-old offspring of line 890, however, were sent directly to the Cavalry School because everybody knew from experience that they were talented jumpers. The above average "power of inheritance" has been preserved in this line until today, and thus the line—though not very well known—serves as an interesting example. One branch of Bizarre has now been preserved in my neighborhood for more than thirty years (for details see the following pages). Inter-

Bizarre H5388165 born 1965 by Cromwell out of Kamille by Maki I

Modesto by Marlon xx born 1970
German Vice Champion under Lene Nissen-Lemke

Historie H66644171

Jula (Cuba) H14341 by Urioso born 1972

Placed first in advanced level competition under Elmar and Alois Pollmann-Schweckhorst, including the Verden Grand Prix, before being exported to Italy.

Nelke (Friona) H6521 by Freeman xx born 1976

Competed to medium level difficulty (3'9" to 4'6").

Ostia (Frimella) H1641 by Freeman xx born 1977

Successful in Nations' Cups and World Cup competitions ridden by Alois Pollmann-Schweckhorst.

Rinka H3451 by Maximus born 1979

Feodora by Farnese
At age seven, she had three wins under Elmar Pollmann-Schweckhorst. Then, in one season she was Regional, German, and European Champion ridden by Fritz Fervers.

Mira by Midas born 1976
Placed at advanced level under Alois Pollmann-Schweckhorst; exported to Sweden.

Tafina H4309135 by Caletto I
Because of an injury, she never competed and was only used as a broodmare.

Vardana by Fernando
Registered for performance; due to injury, never competed.

Carlo by Corvado born 1984
Won at medium level competition (3'9" to 4'6"), placed at advanced level.

Condor by Caletto I born 1980
Won at medium level (3'9" to 4'6") under Elmar Pollmann-Schweckhorst, but died at age eight.

B Legende by Lombard born 1987
Won competitions in Switzerland.

Cap Silver alias "Silvercap" H16681 by Silvester born 1991
International competitions under Axel Fromm.

Born 1998

Stallion by Lord born 1992
Exported to Switzerland.

Animus by Altano born 1988
Won at advanced level under Steffi Radons.

Cappuccino by Caretino born 1989
Auctioned at age three for over $30,000.

Cathleen (ex Coba) H2501 by Caretino born 1990
Competed internationally under Marc Wirths.

Caprice H1852 by Caretino born 1991

Cobblestone's Cookie H22371 by Corrado I born 1992
Placed at advanced; exported to the United States.

Alo's As by Alcatraz born 1993
Winner in classes for young riding horses and, at age six, at intermediate (US level 7).

Mare by Contender born 1999
Federal elite mare, registered in studbook for performance, with marks for jumping ability the maximum "10."

Mare by Contender born 2000

Stallion by Lovaletto born 2001

STANDING 2002

Kentucky's Grundy Lee H2171 by Grundyman xx born 1991

Won several advanced competitions ridden by Sebastian Otten during his apprenticeship with the author.

Kentucky's Cassily by Cassini I

Total index at mare performance test: 9.5; won competition for young horses at US Level 4; at age six and after two foals, she won competition for young horses at intermediate (US Level 7).

Mare by Lavaletto born 1999

Stallion by Calando I born 2000
Exported to Belgium.

Alcagrund by Alcatraz born 1996

Won an intermediate class (US Level 7) for young horses at age five.

Eurocommerce Berlin *alias* **"Caspar" by Cassini born 1994**

Participated in the Federal Championship licensing tests at Adelheidsdorf, placed 2nd in jumping; placed at advanced level; exported to the Netherlands and internationally successful under Wim Schröder.

C'est la Vie by Cassini I born 1997
In her mare performance test, marked "10" for jumping.

Mare by Coriano born 2001

Stallion by Cassini II born 1998

Stallion by Cap born 2001

Mare by Coriano born 2002

national show jumpers such as Corinessa (ridden by Cora Ackermann), Crocodile Dandy (ridden by Alison Firestone), and some stallions graded for stud in Holstein have come out of another branch of this same line (it meets at Bizarre's mother, Kamille).

Certain stallion lines, as well as mare lines, produce jumpers with a higher probability of success than others. Stallion siring abilities are more obvious, and seen on a broader range than that of mares because of the numerous offspring a stallion is able to produce. But, all lines are transitory—no branch blossoms forever. This has to do with more than the fact that breeding aims have changed over the years. A guiding principle when assessing a pedigree is, "Three times nothing, makes nothing." This means that even from the best of families, performance is no longer to be expected after three generations of unskillful crossings.

The personal performance of a horse's ancestors is the next important factor. Of course, the conditions under which any accolades were achieved have to be taken into account (such as rider, course builder, and competitors). There has been no perfect horse in the past, and there is none in existence today—it is likely a successful ancestor was simply lucky enough to meet with favorable circumstances that helped balance his disadvantages. This is one reason why two outstanding parents do not necessarily produce an outstanding foal, though the probability increases if the breed is based on lines and families that have been selected and crossed for the desired traits for many generations.

The Suitable Match

In order to be able to assess a pedigree successfully, the "suitable match" has to be taken into account. The complex term "jumping ability" comprises two main tendencies: one type of horse excels through great scope and courage but tends to be somewhat careless and simple-minded; the other is clever and careful, but with a latent tendency toward a limited scope and a lack of courage. The majority of big horses belong to the first type, whereas among smaller ones, the smart type prevails. Many great jumpers were created by crossing these two main types. Thus there are brilliant sires of jumpers (with strong nerves, great scope, and a willingness to perform) that produce successful offspring only when matched to refined mares (those that are smart, intelligent, and possess stamina). When two parents, although perhaps both very successful in performance possess the same disadvantages, those disadvantages will most probably be intensified in the offspring.

In addition, there are differences due to sex. Among full brothers and sisters, the colts tend to be vigorous and confident bordering on stubborn. Fillies are often a smaller and more refined type, and if they have an extremely female outlook, their behavior is often moody and "mare-ish" as if they were continually in heat. On average, geldings are less complicated and more forgiving with regard to mistakes made by the rider but they often tend to be somewhat ordinary and boring.

Line Breeding

The probability of transmitting certain genes is increased in the case of breeding with related bloodlines (in Germany called *Blutanschluss*, or "blood connection") or when inbreeding is used. But beware! Negative characteristics are, of course, passed down with equal power.[6] Therefore, let me repeat: there never has been, and there never will be a horse that possesses all desired characteristics without any disadvantage. Moreover, the ideal image is always tied to its era. If the ancestors were desirable athletes or sires of successful jumpers in the 1950s or 1960s, the jumping rules and circumstances at that time must be taken into account before line breeding is considered. The athletic standards of both riding and breeding cannot be compared to those of today; the fences were more solid, the jump cups deeper, the poles heavier. For these reasons, a jumper had no need to be as careful.

Conformation

If you want to enjoy jumping, only train horses that are suitable for this discipline in both mind and body. They should basically find pleasure in jumping and should physically measure up to the future task. The ability to assess conformation is important not only in view of anticipated riding qualities but also in potential resistance to injury.

"A horse with harmonious and correct conformation has only to get into the hands of a good rider in order to reach peak performance." This sentence, often repeated by one Rhineland breeding expert, is easily dis-

missed when you watch a championship class. Jumpers of international standing differ so widely in conformation, size, and type that conformation may be considered far less important than inner values. Maas Johannes Hell, the discoverer of numerous exceptionally good jumpers explains, "No horse is too small or too big, but he may be just not good enough."

Nevertheless, there are certain physical characteristics that favor or hinder a horse being considered as a jumper.

Scope and Build

The best jumpers are not coarsely built. Very bony and crude horses are seldom sensitive or smart, and thus are not clever and/or careful enough. (The absolute exception to this was Willi Melliger's giant grey Calvaro; his reflexes at a jump were quite unusual for a horse of his type.) Very refined horses, on the other hand, need a smaller, lightweight rider in order to unfold their abilities. And, even then they do not often actually possess the scope of Joe Fargis' fragile Touch of Class, winner of an Olympic silver medal. In principle, an excellent big horse can jump higher than an excellent small one—not in a relative but in an absolute sense. Nevertheless, there were small horses that achieved incredible successes, and to name just two out of many: Marion Mould's Olympic mount, the Irish pony Stroller, and the Argentine ex-polo pony Zurkis (twice second at the Hamburg Derby under Victor Teixeira).

Equally, the best jumpers are more of a "rectangular" than a "square" type. "Length has to do with scope," says Hans Horn, ex-national trainer of the Netherlands. This

---

[6] Kidd, Jane, *The Horse: The Complete Guide to Horse Breeds and Breeding*, Longmeadow Press, 1993.

perception is not new. During the time of the Cavalry School of Hannover, Major von Busse wrote, "One experience has proven true: in good jumpers, a long back is found much more frequently than a short one. Another thing is the neck—there are real champions with rather short necks."

Horses with very short necks are usually thick through the throatlatch and do not make very comfortable rides. If the neck is long enough but very low set on (often in connection to a ewe-neck) the horse tends to "push into" an obstacle and has difficulty checking his paces before taking off. (Usually, the front legs are not lifted quickly enough from the ground.) On the contrary, horses with highly set necks, such as Hackneys and certain other carriage horse breeds, are often high-stepping and very good at lifting and tucking up their front legs. However, the strongly "uphill" look is caused by the back being hollowed, which makes it difficult for them to bascule over the jump. This type of horse can only desperately fold their hind legs over the jump instead of opening up. Almost all the top international jumpers have a neck that is set on not particularly high or low, and a steep shoulder—somehow, this steep shoulder seems to improve the ability to avoid faults made by the forehand.

Exceptional jumpers are often somewhat higher behind. This is probably because of the "engine" having a bigger dimension. But here, as well, there is a "too much"—the higher a horse is behind and the

"Length impacts scope." Ratina Z's topline and the angles and long lines of her hindquarters show where she got her enormous jumping capacity. She was a classical product of breeding for performance: her sire Ramiro, his dam Coralle (registered name, Valine), her dam's sire Almé, and her grandmother Heureka were all jumpers of international reputation. ▼

▲ *Powerful jumpers are often a bit higher behind, as seen here with Come On. His "engine" has desirably large dimensions. Despite his being higher behind, this Holsteiner stallion always moved in balance because his neck and head were set high, too. Because of this strong, high-set neck and his enormous scope, he hardly ever showed any bascule when jumping.*

▲ *Different conformation, different strong points: the conformation of the stallion Champion du Lys discloses his practical, balanced build, which became apparent in his early maturity. It was not by chance that by the age of six he had won five international competitions at the highest level and was third at the Mexican Derby. Such a horse does not need to be "held together" or balanced by his rider as he is naturally cut out for sport. On the contrary, he actually requires a relatively free canter in order to reach his jumping potential.*

▲ *Caletto I and Grandeur: These two stallions were at the top internationally, both in sport and breeding, although athletic performance does not always guarantee above-average breeding performance. In this photograph, Caletto I looks well fattened, but even in his prime a smart jumper on the competitive circuit, and noticeably short-coupled. Note the sloping croup and the relatively close angles of the hind legs.*

▲ *Grandeur is almost contrary in conformation: longer in the ribs, the hock is placed higher, and the croup is shorter, which emphasizes once again—they win in all shapes and sizes. The expression on Grandeur's face indicates his good nerve, which he proved in numerous competitions both for scope and speed.*

longer his back, the more problems he will have balancing himself. If a horse that is extremely high behind does not show any uphill tendency, even when at liberty, this may also affect his jumping technique. Because he lacks balance and has difficulty checking his paces (collecting himself), he will be prone to faults made by the forehand.

The aim of any breeder of sport horses is good bulk and substance, which is not to be confused with size. For example, a pony may have more bulk and substance than a big Warmblood if, in proportion with his body, the pony has a stronger neck, a longer shoulder, or longer-lined hindquarters. In the case of the jumper, generous substance is favored, though now and again there are top international jumpers with conformation that contradicts this general rule.

Considering jumpers as a whole, the "careful" ones often show a big, clear, somewhat bulging eye. In my opinion, this not only provides a wider visual angle but also reflects attentiveness.

Some time ago it was maintained that there were no outstanding jumpers "with high hocks,"[7] or, that "the elbow should stand out from the rib cage one-hand's-breadth" in order to make the horse more sure-footed. Perhaps it is due to the change of basic conditions (obstacles, course design, level of riding, and ground conditions) that today, no connection can be found between these characteristics and jumping talent.

Toughness and Resistance

Conformation may also give information on other aspects of suitability: for example, the skeletal construction of the horse allows

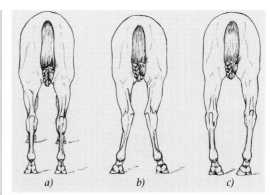

a) correct
b) cow-hocked
c) bow-legged

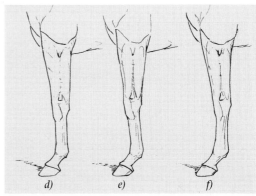

d) correct, well-shaped forelegs
e) over at the knee
f) back at the knee

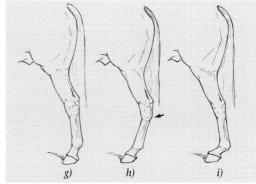

g) correct hind leg
h) strongly angulated hind leg with curb (see arrow)
i) very straight (open) hind leg with long, soft (steeply angled) pastern

---

[7] Nissen, Jasper, *Springen und was dazu gehört* (Jumping and who it belongs to), Heidenheim: E. Hoffmann Verlag, 1968 (p. 51).

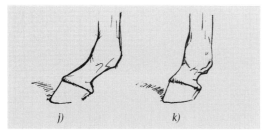

j) long, soft (steeply angled)) pastern
k) short, upright pastern

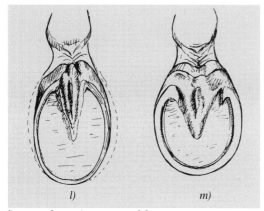

l) narrow foot   m) correct round foot

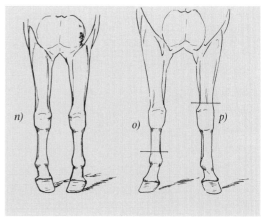

n) pigeon-toed
o) turned out from the fetlock joint (see line)
p) turned out from the knee (see line)

conclusions to be drawn about his ability to resist stress. Let us begin with the bridge between the forehand and the hindquarters: the back. A "soft" top line is often suspected to cause back problems, but this has not been confirmed. Damage to the dorsal vertebrae where the saddle lies is more often caused by a high head and neck carriage, tension, or a lack of preparedness for the increased stress of competition. When a horse is collected or when he lands after a jump, the spinal processes tend to touch if the muscles get weak and tired because of excess strain. Then any concussion and vibrations must be compensated by the skeleton and the ligaments.[8] However, a back capable of bearing weight is vital for the ability of the hindquarters to create impulsion that can flow freely through the whole body, and a horse with a "solid" top line tends to jump more powerfully—more "through his body." (An example of a soft back that did not hinder a top international career is Calido, ridden by the Norwegian Geir Gulliksen at the 2001 European Championship.)

As regards the legs: faulty conformation of the fore and/or hind limbs, such as forelegs that are markedly pigeon-toed, toed-out, or clearly back at the knee, or hind legs that are cow-hocked or bow-legged, represent real disadvantages with regard to resistance to stress and strain (inflamed tendons, bone spavins, and the like). Of course, this depends on the degree of the defects.

Renowned breeding expert Werner Schockemöhle explains, "Whenever there is a 'slightly' in front of the conformation fault, it is a pardonable sin, but when there is a 'too' in front, it has to be considered a fault that would reduce the life span or permanently impair the riding quality of the horse, and thus should be regarded as a mortal sin."

---

[8] Friedrich, Gabriele, *Die Erkrankungen des Sportpferdes* (The ailments of sport horses), Warendorf: FN-Verlag, 1986 (pp. 64-67).

Moreover, he indicates that conformation faults such as incorrect position of limbs or sway or hollow back have a tendency to increase with age. Also of importance is the kind of fault in question; "over at the knee" has never ended a jumping career prematurely. On the other hand, "soft" (too sloping) pasterns affect the ligaments as well as the navicular region, and steep pasterns put strain on the joints, especially in the forelegs because there is not enough resilience when the foot strikes the ground.

The shape of the foot is considered of vital importance. It should correspond to the bulk and size of the horse and must not be too small. Only a foot of sufficient size that widens toward the ground like a funnel has enough room for a healthy frog, and provides the necessary blood supply to the navicular region. A narrow hoof or a poorly defined frog have a causal relation to navicular disease, and a flat hoof puts strain on the navicular region and the tendons, especially when it is pushed or "rolled" off (the movement between putting the foot down and lifting it up again; in humans, this is the moment when the foot touches the ground from heel to toe). Contracted heels cause increased pressure on the heels, which tend to sink in deeper when landing after the jump. This, in turn, causes extreme stress on the region of the pedal bone and the superficial tendons.

Although Warmblood breeders try to fight such heritable faults through selective breeding (by means of stallion grading and broodmare shows), no Warmblood breed can do without Thoroughbred blood—and in Thoroughbred breeding, only racing performance decides which horses are going to stud. Horses with a high percentage of Thoroughbred blood tend to have conformational issues with their hocks, which makes them prone to developing a curb. Very flat hocks may promote bone spavin. (These should be regarded as weaknesses only if they are due to excess strain, not if they are inherited.[9])

A jumper should show stamina and resistance to stress. These criteria (admittedly subjective) cannot solely be tied to correct conformation and good upbringing, nor can they be determined by a veterinarian. A pre-purchase vet check can provide information on anomalies seen in X rays or acute diseases, but not about the horse's real resistance to stress or the length of time the animal will be usable. These have to be evaluated by the rider. Indications may be "clean" legs without swellings and lumps, and more importantly, feet that are put down in a determined and rhythmical way, even without a warm-up, and even on hard ground and in turns.

Disposition and "Heart"

The term "disposition" is comprised of more than character and temperament. For example, "endurance" is also an inner value of a horse. It is probably due to different levels of tolerance to pain that some horses, despite poor X rays, yield top performances up to the age of seventeen or eighteen, whereas others endure only one or two years although they have not been exposed to excessive stress.

A good example is the horse that has endured a long haul to a show, coming off the trailer a bit "foot sore" and tired, but still managing to overcome the stress of the trip and jump well when asked, with energy and

[9] Nissen, Jasper, *Springen und was dazu gehört* (Jumping and who it belongs to), Heidenheim: E. Hoffmann Verlag, 1968 (p. 56).

27

eagerness. The opposite is the horse who allows himself to succumb to his weariness, and it is this "soft" type that only lasts for a limited time in the world of jumping.

Temperament

Besides an eagerness to go forward, a good temperament should also be comprised of a good "nerve." The ideal jumper is sensitive, but nevertheless robust and of equable temperament. Of course, there are exceptions to the rule. In the daily routine, high-spirited horses may need more time and may cause more problems, but when competing, they often excel because of their fighting spirit and endurance. Helena Weinberg, one of the best female riders in the world, explains:

> *I like horses to be a little vivacious. I've never met one that would have been too "hot" for me...If a horse is very high-spirited the only question is how to manage him. The warm-up is done differently, the daily flatwork at home is done a bit differently, and I don't insist on things that are apt to make such a horse react violently.*
>
> *The Hannoveraner, 7/76*, August, 2002

The nerve of more stolid horses allows them to win more frequently because they do not tend to get frantic or lose control during a round. But, in most cases they do not develop the same fighting morale as a high-spirited horse of the same quality. They give in sooner if things get difficult. High-spirited horses tend to deal with challenges more easily once they have warmed up to the occasion.

Aperio's dam Fulda and ▶
Alois Pollmann-Schweckhorst, Junior.

Character

Good horses not only "can," they also "want to." Willingness to perform is an important prerequisite for a prospective jumper. But, horses with strong personalities occasionally show little readiness to submit to the will of a rider, especially one who is less strong. As strong characters are often found among top horses, the rider needs to pay special attention in order to avoid fighting with the horse—in particular, he needs to give clear aids, and avoid overtraining.

Performance horses are often complicated animals. For the jumping course, we are looking for an athlete with fighting spirit. Thus we must not complain if this willfulness has not yet been sufficiently channelled

Chapter 2

when training begins, and if it sometimes works against the rider. With the right measure of discipline, perseverance, and reward these horses may develop into exceptional athletes.

Strong-willed horses are not everybody's ride. They need a firm and safe hand to guide them as uncertainty, inconsistency, or injustice on the rider's part is met with disobedience far more quickly than from the average riding horse.

However, these headstrong characters should not be confused with horses lacking in sporting spirit. If a horse lacks the right attitude from the start, not even a strong rider can overcome it for long. The problem will recur, and in my experience, such a horse does not remain in the competitive scene.

It is quite a different matter if, in the beginning, a horse tends to be "spooky." It is normal for young horses to be suspicious of new things, and this natural shyness and

apprehensiveness suggests alertness and caution—characteristics a rider should appreciate. Suspicion toward everything new is a heightened form of attentiveness and a natural instinct that has been responsible for the horse's survival for millions of years. Many top jumpers (such as Deister, Fire, Priamos, De Niro, and Aperio) tended to spook—if not for their entire lives, then at least in the beginning of their careers. Horses like these will become more confident when the rider remains calm.

Providing variety in daily training and encouraging calmness in the ring also helps. As trust and experience increase, this bad habit often subsides. Keeping future jumpers according to their natural requirements (with a lot of exercise) also aids in the development of good nerves. If, however, this habit remains a permanent problem even though the rider does not provoke a fight (and during the warm-up is willing to overlook it) the horse may just have a spooky character. The question then is whether the horse is really suitable for jumping at all. There is nothing more frustrating for a trainer than to be eliminated from an important competition because, even after years of patient schooling, his horse suddenly dislikes some flower pot. Very spooky horses are—as a rule—not worth the long-term commitment of training and schooling.

Aperio's dam Fulda was trained by my father, and she had a strong-willed personality. When young, her tendency to be headstrong was especially apparent: if my father applied spurs to assist her in front of a parallel, she would soar over the spread and stop dead in her tracks immediately after landing. Not one more step would she go. But, her jumping technique was so outstanding that my father put up with it. In the course of time, she became more tolerant and more submissive, and he was able to win his last competition with her. Thereafter, my brother took over and was reserve champion and third at the European Championships in Donaueschingen, Germany.

Free Jumping

Until the middle of the twentieth century, free jumping was considered a regular training method. For this reason, in the thirties the Cavalry School of Hannover owned a free jumping course consisting of a high-fenced, oval pathway with different obstacles and grids set at varying distances. Horses were let loose to jump the course by themselves, which was thought to improve their ability to organize their stride and arrive at the correct spot for takeoff. This training method was the natural consequence of a jumping technique that did not try to control the point of takeoff (a style that was last represented internationally by Mexican riders in the forties and fifties).

In the years that followed, the point of takeoff was more and more controlled by the rider. Course designers gradually agreed on uniform standard distances. The number of strides was strictly calculated. Where professional show jumping was concerned, it suddenly became undesirable for horses to look for the correct takeoff point by themselves, so free jumping was reduced to a method of examining green horses for jumping talent.

Evidence of Ability

Free jumping provides the first evidence of a horse's jumping ability to riders and breeders. At stallion gradings, broodmare shows, and sales, free jumping is a very important selective criterion. But be careful: not every "artistic" free jumper makes a good jumper under saddle, and some top international show jumpers made a very poor impression when free jumped in their youths. Helena Weinberg, international show jumper and horse trader, agrees to this:

Some horses exhibit quite different jumping styles when free jumping compared to jumping under saddle. Jumping is a ridden sport, and, of course, two-year-old horses cannot be assessed other than by free jumping. Many early "power" jumpers are never seen later on in competition. Small horses that perhaps free jump with much agility and technique but without much power because they are careful, don't call much attention to themselves but later, at the age of six, seven, or eight appear in the show jumping arenas.

The Hannoveraner, 7/76, August, 2002

Free jumping has its own rules. Young horses that fulfill the most difficult requirements with the calmness and confidence of experienced jumpers often lose respect for rails after some years of training under saddle. Others, careful horses, often present themselves in a shy and hesitating manner during their first free-jumping sessions, and their qualities only become visible later when they have gained confidence after being trained by good riders and gaining some experience.

◀ *Aperio at the age of four, free jumping an airy spread and fully demonstrating his qualities. His style has remained to today: relaxed hindquarters and well tucked-up forelegs, forearms at or below the horizontal, and little bascule.*

▲ *Ratina Z's free jumping did not hint to anybody that she was to become the most successful show jumper in the world. Because of her keen temperament and her physical conformation, she made little use of her body when free jumping and tended to jump too much forward. Careful schooling by excellent riders finally transformed these weaknesses into a special advantage.*

At sales today, three-year-old horses are offered as potential "champions" for dressage, eventing, or show jumping based on the belief that these hardly backed horses will at some time excel in the respective disciplines. This is pure nonsense. The experts know that it is a long way from basic schooling to top performance and a way that requires much patience.

DR. REINER KLIMKE
(1936-1999)

Nevertheless, free jumping can provide important information for the assessment of horses not yet backed, though you should not expect the same ability to be demonstrated as from a fully trained jumper. It is often more telling how a young horse jumps a small fence than how he jumps an enormous spread. Moreover, I recommend taking into account the points described on the following pages:

Construction of the Grid

The position of the indoor arena entrance and exit is of vital importance when free jumping. Young horses often feel isolated in an indoor arena and are attracted by the exit, so in the beginning, it is helpful to have them jump *toward* the exit. Horses with some experience and an excess amount of eagerness, however, show more deliberation when jumping in the opposite direction (*away* from the exit). It is not advised to position the exit at the side of the grid. In this case, some horses tend to lose impulsion and do not "finish" their jumps.

In my opinion, it depends on the construction of the indoor arena and the type of horse whether jumping the grid is done clockwise or counterclockwise. Some trainers think that horses prefer jumping to the left, but this may also be due to the fact that most people are right-handed and, therefore, prefer holding the whip in their right hand.

In big arenas it is advisable to train horses over a grid in order to control them and prevent them from gaining too much speed. A row of obstacles can be totally fenced-in on one side by high "wings" (these should be significantly higher than the jumps so that running out is not an option). Then, for better control of pace, horses are led toward the first jump and (depending on their temperament) released 16 to 30 feet (5 to 10m) before. I recommend doubling the lead rope and pulling the resulting loop through the bit ring from the inside out. Then the loop and the two ends of the rope are held with the fore- and middle fingers. To release the horse, you simply let the loop slip through the bit ring, and the flow of motion is not interrupted.

The wing should have a small gap between it and the fence so the handler can take action at all times if needed. When the grid ends toward the wall of the arena make sure there is enough space so the horse doesn't hesitate before the final jump.

Grids are especially recommended for horses that have already garnered some experience free jumping over single fences. Usually these grids consist of three fences, and only the third element varies in its dimensions—the first two are meant to control the rhythm and pace and the point of takeoff. For the same reason, a distance of one canter stride between fences is preferred, though horses with a tendency to rush their fences can be encouraged to jump more deliberately by placing poles between the fences. The last fence is usually a spread, and to better evaluate a jumper's quality, it is recommended to let him jump this last element first as a spread and then change it to a vertical. The massive construction of a spread (a red and white triple bar, for example) may make the horse's foreleg technique appear quicker and better than it really is, so for accurate assessment, a simple construction and naturally colored poles are recommended.

When watching a horse free jumping, the qualities you are looking for depend, of course, on what you are planning do with him. An amateur rider may find it interesting to have the horse jump a simple fence without a ground line in order to have an idea of the horse's ability to see his strides. In every case, a quiet and relaxed atmosphere is vital in order to be able to see the potential of a jumper.

Assessment under Saddle

When trying a horse under saddle, you want to assess his qualities as reliably as possible. It has proven to be quite efficient for a rider to first test basic dressage skills (according to the Training Scale) and then try to come to a basic agreement with the horse. Gaps in his education can sometimes be overcome with more schooling, but this should not tempt you to think (and hope) that "As soon as he is really worked with, he will jump much better!" Remember, it is wise to only pay for what you actually see.

Rideability

Inborn rideability is a "must" for horses challenged by the technical requirements of today's jumping courses. Such horses will eventually respond to their riders' aids without resistance even under difficult conditions.

Good-natured, uncomplicated horses cause few problems; however, they often lack the certain desirable "esprit" (spirit). Horses with fighting spirit, often preferred by professionals, can be fractious when young and quick to resist their riders. Empathy and patient flatwork are required in these cases. Such horses must be worked with the aim of compensating for their weaknesses without harping on them. Keep in mind that there is no horse without faults—the aim is to strengthen good qualities and compensate for the bad. But, for the ambitious competitive rider, it holds sadly true what Franke Sloothaak aptly phrased, "You can live with one problem, but with two you are already out of the money."

Basic Paces

A young or untrained horse may be forgiven if he is not very light-footed, for in the course of schooling, this can be improved with gymnastic exercises that develop propulsion and carrying forces. If a trained horse still moves clumsily and awkwardly, he is sure to lack the ultimate "knack" when jumping.

The trot is interesting when assessing a potential jumper because it provides the first impression of the horse's strength and toughness. However, it does not tell much about jumping talent. There may be a certain connection between a buoyant, high-stepping action and a quick foreleg technique, or between a flatter trot and poor folding of the forelegs, but few older, successful jumpers show a buoyant, trot. A "short" trot may indicate wear and tear, but it is frequently due to the fact that there is no effort made to develop a spectacular trot in jumpers. Trotting is done for the sake of suppleness, not for "showy" purposes, and many an expressive trot is literally eliminated in the course of jumping work.

A long-striding walk usually indicates a big canter, and a big canter stride is closely connected to "scope" in jumping. The canter can be easily assessed in a one-stride combination. For the jumper, the canter is the most important gait. It should be round, fluid, light-footed, and long-striding (a forward-and-upward movement) with propulsion from the hind end. When the center of gravity is shifted more toward the head (on the forehand), it can result in poor foreleg jumping technique. Moreover, a horse like this has difficulty compensating for awkward jumping distances by quickly inserting a small canter stride. And, a horse with a high neck and a hollow back may be better at shortening his stride, but has more difficulty basculing and "opening up" over a jump.

Good riders who want to ride at higher levels can put up initially with a too big canter stride because it can be controlled by proper schooling. However, a "chicken stride" cannot be overcome.

Careful Tendency

A horse with a big canter stride that gives the impression of being a bit timid and careful, but is intelligent, may confidently be taken and trained even if he does not yet show maximum scope. His scope will improve in proportion to the trust he gains with a competent rider over the years of training. On the other hand, a horse that, at the age of four or five, boldly jumps advanced-level fences but does so with the coolness of an experienced, older horse should be regarded with suspicion. After a few years he may lack respect for jumps with rails. All of this adds up to the fact that you may be able to compromise with regard to his canter stride and scope as long as he is careful and accurate.

Fair Testing

It makes sense to test a horse for an amateur by setting up "exaggerated" distances—very far off or close to a fence. However, a horse for a more advanced rider can be ridden at medium speed and minimal rider influence to the ideal takeoff point. This enables the rider to assess the horse's basic abilities. If he uses more influence, it could possibly hide a lack of courage on the part of the horse, or make his forehand technique appear better than it really is. Riding to an awkward takeoff point can provoke a surprise or challenge, which might lead a less careful horse to show better reflexes than usual, but a "quality" horse might tense and present himself in poor light.

It should be understood that condition and level of training must be taken into

▲ After Gralshüter (sire owned by the North Rhine Westfalian state stud in Warendorf, Germany) was systematically trained by a level-headed rider (Heinrich-Wilhelm Johannsmann), he was capable of jumping fences that early in his career, nobody believed he ever would. In today's sport, a cautious and handy horse is worth more than an outstanding power jumper that lacks cleverness. The international courses with their light construction and intense technical requirements are made for clever, careful horses, even if they do not possess that last bit of scope. Unfortunately, jumpers that were considered of ideal type in the seventies have very few occasions where they can still successfully participate.

account when a horse is tried out. A horse trader can set up an array of deceptions, which may not be immediately apparent. A buyer—as careful as he may be—can never entirely safeguard himself against tricks. Often, it is important to consider who is offering the horse for sale and what the horse's career was up to that time. It may also be interesting to inquire about the conditions under which any competitive successes took place. There are marked regional differences as to course design and quality of participant performance.

Most important, however, is that the horse fits the rider—physically and mentally. Therefore, when looking for a horse, first look at yourself!

Chapter 3

Dressage for Jumpers

For performance potential to be totally developed, more than riding plays a role. The whole "package" must be right. It is in basic schooling that undreamed-of qualities are developed—or irreparable damage is done.

What factors affect a jumper's ability?

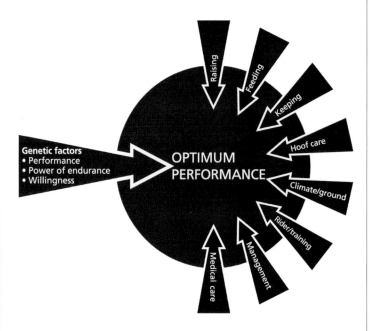

Genetic factors
• Performance
• Power of endurance
• Willingness

OPTIMUM PERFORMANCE

Raising
Feeding
Keeping
Hoof care
Climate/ground
Rider/training
Management
Medical care

Fitness Training

Genetic abilities can only be developed by continuous and constructive training. Requirements that are gradually and repeatedly increased will improve perform-ance. The effects of such training may be divided into two categories:

1. By training the *muscular* system, power, speed, and endurance are improved.
2. By training the *nervous* system, agility, locomotion, and concentration are improved.

Especially during the first stages of schooling, the main aim—besides cognitive and motor-coordinative training—should be responsiveness to the aids. During the first few years, the horse's system trains itself via new and unusual exercises. One hour of riding a day with half an hour of walking before and after (for the benefit of blood circulation and the loosening of the muscles) creates sufficient condition to suc-cessfully jump a medium-level difficulty course—a course between 984' and 1,148' (300m to 350m) with eight to fourteen fences at heights of 3' 9" to 4' 6" (1.20m to 1.40m). This level does not constitute a real challenge for a modern Warmblood.

When the jumper has learned his ABCs, he has "only" to be kept in shape. Apart from occasional gymnastic exercises or schooling special problems, jumping in competition is enough for him to stay in condition.

The muscular system of the horse adapts to increased stress within a few weeks. The rider may be tempted by this fact to set tasks for a talented and willing horse after a relatively short time of training as he would to an experienced competition horse. But, tendons, bones, and ligaments (as well as the horse's mind) need to be built up over a longer, continuous phase in order for them to become resistant to stress down the road. With a young horse, emphasis is on improving responsiveness to the aids, technique, concentration, and quick reactions. "Technical abilities are achieved by continually practicing the movements...and include a learning process based on the engraining of *reflexes*."[10]

This does not only apply to jump training, but also to flatwork. The main aim is to create the conditions for a maximum performance in competition. While jumping a course, the horse should give a picture of efficiency, lightness, and harmony. To create this impression, discreet aids are necessary, which are based on dressage work and mutual agreement between horse and rider.

The Rider's Training Scale

A rider has to pass through various stages of schooling himself before he is able to train a horse properly. He must be able to successfully adapt to diverse characters and problems, which requires more than just talent. Nothing makes learning easier for a young horse than an experienced "jockey" on his back. And, nothing can upset him more quickly than an inexperienced rider.

Young riders on experienced horses, experienced riders on young horses!

In my opinion the rider's Training Scale is not completely covered by the description "seat—aids—feeling—influence." A more detailed explanation could be as follows:

Riding a schooled horse:
● Knowledge of seat and movement
● Feeling for seat and movement
● Knowledge of aids and techniques
● Feeling for the use of aids and techniques
● **Result: Influence**

Schooling a young horse:
● Knowledge of physiology, psychology, and natural history of the horse
● Feeling for condition, state of development, and potential of a horse
● **Result: Horsemanship**

In practice, the transitions between the stages are seamless because most riders (assisted by experienced trainers) should start working with young horses relatively early. A certain talent and lots of hard work are essential in order to make this a success.

Empathy—combined with determination—is perhaps the most important talent a good rider should possess. Without this feeling for the horse or the situation at hand, no theoretical edifice of thought is of any value. But, without theoretical knowledge the rider can only proceed according to a "trial-and-error" method and is destined to lose much time as a consequence.

The basics of classical dressage apply to all disciplines and are valid at all times. They are the most proven way for developing the potential of any horse. For this reason, the training of a jumper is described here in accordance with the theoretical model of schooling in dressage.

---

[10] Launer, Miller, and Richter, *Krankheiten des Reitpferdes* (Diseases of the riding horse), Verlag Eugen Ulmer, 1990 (pp. 74—76).

It is true that riding is a science; any science is based on principles, and doctrines are absolutely essential because anything really good and beautiful cannot be based on accident.

EARL OF PEMBROKE

Dressage for Jumpers vs. Competitive Dressage

Dressage for jumpers concentrates on different aspects than dressage for competition. For example, expressive movements of vital importance to a dressage horse are insignificant for a jumper. In dressage competition, a relatively rigid protocol has to be fulfilled. Trainers and judges have an exact idea of how every single movement should be executed, and this concept is the criterion for judging. In show jumping, the ultimate measure is the fastest round without faults, regardless of any antics in between.

Nevertheless, the basic elements are the same for both. Competitive dressage and dressage for jumpers are two branches of the same tree. It is even quite possible to achieve a state of collection in jumping similar to that of competitive dressage. The big difference is in the duration and intensity of high collection and in the aim for cadence. A cadenced rhythm (for example, a prolonged phase of suspension) is of no use to a jumper.

In this chapter, the training of the modern jumper is explained on the basis of the dressage system. But, from the beginning, this flatwork aimed at basic schooling is accompanied by jumping exercises. As soon as the horse has learned to carry a rider, he can be ridden over a ground pole. Not very much later, a small fence can be jumped from the trot (at first, without a distracting trotting pole in front), maybe with another horse in the lead in order to make use of the herd instinct. Jumping is a totally natural movement for horses, and jump work progresses along with development in dressage.

Unorthodox Ideas on the Training Scale

The Training Scale is a logical and systematic classification of the individual training sections and schooling stages followed in developing a dressage horse. The Scale is meant for short-term goals—such as the structure of a schooling session—as well as for medium- and long-term schooling. The concept of the Training Scale and its aims

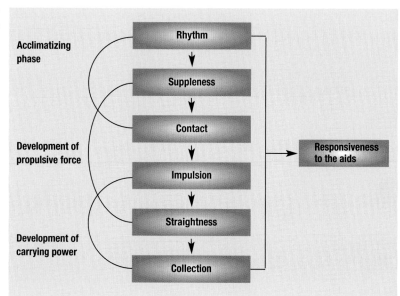

are recognised and appreciated throughout the world, and any serious dressage for jumpers is based—whether consciously or unconsciously—on this scheme because the tasks and problems presented by modern course designers cannot be solved by ability alone.

But, even the committee that determined the Training Scale disagreed on the order of the individual subjects, and this order remains a point of discussion today. During the last few years, another issue has appeared: the hierarchical structure of the Scale does not really comply with the realities of daily practice.

■ Different Perspectives

Without any doubt, the elements of the Scale are the cornerstones of schooling. Every session, every correction, is first focused on the crucial points of rhythm, suppleness, and contact, followed by the improvement of impulsion, straightness, and collection.

This hierarchical order is correct as a general guideline for schooling. But in daily work, the elements are practiced side by side or in connection with each other from the beginning. As soon as he rides the first circle, the rider aims for rhythm, contact, and perhaps even straightness. The first full halt works toward collection. Each individual principle can only be improved via the others. It might, therefore, be useful to have a second perspective in order to be able to grasp the significance of the Scale as a whole—something like a bird's eye view of all the principles, showing them side by side and of equal importance so they can be seen "flowing" together. The other perspective—the "sideways" perspective, which empha-sizes the hierarchical order—raises further questions.

■ Rhythm before Suppleness?

Rhythm is in first place because it is generally maintained that no schooling step, and no lesson can be right if rhythm is lost during the process. But could not this argument also apply to suppleness? Some people say rhythm should be addressed first because it is easier to assess. Is this really a sound argument? Time and again, although there are a few efficient dressage riders who are able to hide flaws in suppleness, there are certain clear signs of tension (facial expression, activity of the back, and tail carriage, to name a few), indicating discomfort due to lack of suppleness.

Supporters of the traditional order state that rhythm is the first concept that a rider seeks to improve. Is this right? I would like to quote from the book *Den richtigen Draht finden* (Finding the right connection) by the experienced rider and trainer Christian Pläge, "With regard to rhythm one has to be aware that regular footfalls can only be expected if, by means of suppleness, a state of inner calmness has been reached." If this is true, then shouldn't suppleness be positioned before rhythm?

Let's look at a practical example: a young horse that did not have any exercise the previous day is led under saddle into the indoor arena. He snorts, lifts his tail over his back, and jogs along with buoyant steps instead of walking. His lack of suppleness (and its negative influence on rhythm) is in this case due to a lack of exercise and maybe too much grain, and likely only requires an efficient rider, and in the future, a change in his management and exercise regimen.

In another example, a sensitive mare tenses up because she has been handled roughly or backed too quickly, and now she shows restricted movement or jigs along. In short, she does not move in the required rhythm. In this case, would an experienced horseman really put his emphasis first on rhythm, or would he first try to improve her inner suppleness? He would show he understands her, praise her, and eliminate her distrust and discomfort in order to achieve regular movements by means of *improved suppleness*. Suppleness is rooted in the management framework (such as the horse's handling and living conditions) and results from a basic mutual trust between horse and rider. It forms the bridge between stable and riding arena.

Is it not also true that external suppleness—muscles that tense and relax naturally and have a good and unrestricted blood supply—is the precondition of any further schooling? Does it not accompany all steps of the Scale? What would a regular footfall without suppleness (if this is at all possible) be worth? If suppleness is defined as the *mental* as well as *physical* prerequisite of developing performance, in my opinion, it has to be given the first position in a theoretical hierarchy of thought. According to Knopfhart, "...responsiveness to the aids could be defined as the higher stage of suppleness."[11] This emphasizes that schooling is performed within an arc, which extends from initial trust to eventual responsiveness to the aids. Suppleness and responsiveness to the aids are alpha and omega of the Training Scale.

■ Impulsion before Straightness?

Another inconsistency: impulsion is considered before straightness, but how should a horse develop impulsion if crookedness allows part of his power to pass to one side of his center of gravity and fall flat? Do not both sides of the horse need to be symmetrically strengthened by straightening exercises? Is optimum development of impulsion at all possible without straightness? In my opinion, it is illogical.

In this context, a misleading expression demands our attention. Is it not a linguistic paradox if a horse should be "straightened" even if he is laterally bent? I think that "straightness" should better be replaced by "alignment" (of the forehand with the hindquarters) as the success of "straightening" work is shown not only on straight, but also on bent lines. Of course, there is always professional terminology with significance that must be learned and understood, but does it not hold true that general comprehensiveness is improved by clear and unequivocal terms?

Further, the Scale's division into the *acclimatizing* phase and the development of *propulsive force* and *carrying power* phases is not altogether logical. Is it really sensible to exclude rhythm and collection from the development of propulsion? When impulsion without rhythm gives evidence of a lack of suppleness? Also known is the classical principle, "Extension is the result of collection." And, at the same time extension tells us whether collected work has been executed in the right way. In this case, should not collection be regarded as an element in the development of the propulsive force? Is it not true that propulsion, as well as impulsion, are only perfect if the horse has learned from collected work "to stay on his legs" even in the extended paces? And, is not the carrying power also based on "suppleness, rhythm,

[11] Knopfhart, Alfred, *Fundamentals of Dressage,* New York: Hyperion Books, 1990.

and contact"? Would it be of any value for the training of horses without them?

Alternative Scale

The following diagram may be a better illustration of the interplay of the Training Scale without altogether giving up the hierarchical order of the main principles.

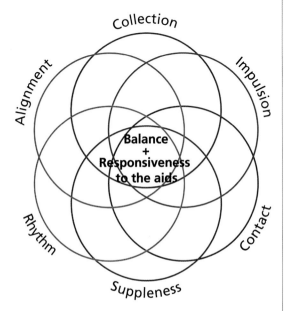

▲ *Could this be the future Training Scale? Looking at this diagram one can imagine a second dimension: the bird's eye view shows how all these points interlock equally. When viewed as on p. 38, the hierarchical order is emphasized. In this case, the order of the focal points is from bottom to top, suppleness being the starting point.*

Among experts, it is quite common to complain about difficulty in understanding the Training Scale. I think that a revision would offer the opportunity of making it more logical and thus more comprehensible. When criticizing the Scale, the object is not to sacrifice well-proven thoughts for new ones. On the contrary; it is precisely because the Training Scale's basic structure has proven sufficiently stable and valuable that it should be revised and thus become standard for future decades. We can only strive to come as close to the truth as possible.

The fact that the order still remains valid despite certain contradictions is probably due to the following reasons:

1. The discussion is of a more theoretical nature. The inconsistencies of the order are not as conspicuous in practical life because eventually the principles interlock. If one step is to be improved it is only possible via the others.

2. Every horse is different. Most have innate problems with some of the principles in the Scale, whereas with others the concepts come so easily they are hardly noticed. The expert rider sets different priorities for each horse. He may make deviations from the order for an individual horse.

3. In practice it is agreed that without any doubt, all elements of the Scale are the basic pillars of schooling. The different models of thought—order or no—end with one aim, which is accepted and strived for by all: an obedient, unconstrained, and harmonious reaction to the rider's aids, optimizing balance and responsiveness among other characteristics.

Because of these reasons, the established order of the Scale (as the official doctrine valid today) is retained for further explanation.

Rhythm

Our German term for beat or rhythm, *Takt,* is derived from the Latin *tactus,* meaning "the beat." It is defined as "a regular beat or the regular change between emphasis and no emphasis." For the movements of the horse, it means the natural change from lifting a foot forward and putting it down again. The measure of the desired rhythm is the natural form of the gait (four-beat, two-beat, or three-beat). In the course of training, rhythm should be found and strengthened, perhaps even optimized.

Faulty rhythm can be divided into four categories:

- Sluggish
- Rushed
- Irregular (short/long movements)
- Jigging (jogging)

Some people maintain that sluggish or rushed movements may nevertheless be rhythmic. I like the term "rhythm" to comprise more than this in order to do justice to its significance in schooling. Both sluggish and rushed movements are evidence of a lack of responsiveness to the aids.

◼ Rhythm in the Basic Paces

Walk is a four-beat gait by nature. It is difficult to improve by riding, but easy to spoil. Horses with a very long-strided walk will sometimes show a tendency to become lateral, even when led in-hand. Many riders consider the walk insignificant in a jumper, but potential problems regarding responsiveness to the aids (leading to problems when riding a course) can often be detected in the walk. Only a calm walk with a rhyth-mic flow of motion through the horse's entire body radiates both composure and dynamic force, making walking important for the suppleness and concentration of the jumper.

Defects in the two-beat *trot* in an otherwise sound horse are due to schooling (mostly a lack of suppleness or instability of contact). Irregular strides during changes of speed may indicate poorly developed propulsive and carrying forces. For jumpers, trotting is mainly used to loosen up and work on lateral bending. It improves rhythm and builds power by developing impulsion. This also makes it good preliminary work for a springy, athletic canter stride.

Nature has designated the *canter* a three-beat gait (when accelerated to the *gallop,* the diagonal pair of legs, which normally strikes the ground simultaneously, does so with a small delay, making the gallop a four-beat gait). A four-beat canter always indicates poor engagement of the hindquarters, which is the rider's fault—he did not pay enough attention to keeping the hindquarters active during training.

Canter is the most important because it is the gait from which tasks have to be solved when jumping a course. An active, rhythmic, light-footed, "uphill" canter makes it easier for the rider to approach an obstacle at the right stride. Occasionally, there are excellent jumpers with a poor canter, and as soon as the rider tries to rate them, their legs seem to knot up. (This is not necessarily due to a lack of suppleness, but may be a kind of physical handicap.) When a horse has a particular talent for jumping, many riders try to compensate for this with skillful riding, and in such cases, the rider adjusts by increasing his forward driving aids and gaining influence just before taking off.

During the 1970s and 1980s, some top international riders from the United States and Canada allowed their horses to go in a four-beat (slow) canter with the aim of relaxing their state of mind. The reason may have been that American jumper riders often learned on Thoroughbreds, and this type of horse has difficulty achieving "inner suppleness," which is as important for them as responsiveness to the aids is for Warmbloods.

There are more excitable types to be found among the refined breeds than among Warmbloods (breeds that, as a rule, are strong-willed and diligent), and the key to a high-spirited horse is indeed a rider who tries to calm him down. The influence of the rider on rhythm can be in an activating as well as a soothing sense, depending on the requirements, as sometimes, there are phlegmatic horses that must be asked for cooperation in a very firm way. These lazy types should be influenced toward a more diligent rhythm, whereas overeager horses should be "turned down" a notch.

In the long run, the American method of neglecting rhythm did not prove successful. This was probably partly due to the fact that more and more European Warmbloods were used overseas for jumping. In addition, course designers developed a tendency toward tricky distances, which demanded responsive horses, and there is no true responsiveness to the aids without rhythm.

Beat and Rhythm in Jumper Training

When jumping, what are the consequences of a poor beat? For one, it is difficult for the rider to get a horse with too-quiet, sluggish movement "in front of him"—the horse does not develop impulsion and is out of balance. On the other hand, rapid movement accompanies a lack of suppleness and results in the horse rushing his fences in a panicky way. Besides suppleness and contact, a "regular beat" is one of the main aims of basic schooling. Young jumpers should be worked simultaneously in both dressage and jumping. In the beginning, simple fences are jumped from the trot, later followed by an easy grid or row of fences at suitable distances (maybe with canter-stride poles in between) in order to transfer the regular beat of the canter to the jump.

The term "rhythm" is derived from the Greek *rhein* meaning "to flow" and signifies the joining together of chronological processes to form a new figure—a whole. This term is used often in jumping as the term *Takt* (beat) alone does not always apply to everything it is meant to cover. On the one hand, the beat of the canter is interrupted by the process of jumping (it adds another phase of suspension between the diagonal pair of hooves striking the ground more or less simultaneously). On the other, a course consists of many canter strides of different lengths. Even if the canter strides are all a correct three-beats, they may be lacking in rhythm—rhythm becomes evident from supple and inconspicuous changes of speed and an uninterrupted flow of motion. Whereas *Takt* describes how the hooves strike the ground and are lifted again within certain recurrent motions (the canter stride, for instance) the term "rhythm" not only means the regular flow of motion while jumping a single fence, but also a whole round.

As soon as the horse is able to continue cantering at medium speed, the first fences

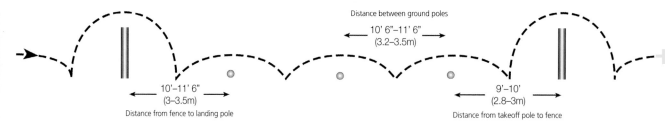

Distance between ground poles
10' 6"–11' 6"
(3.2–3.5m)

10'–11' 6"
(3–3.5m)
Distance from fence to landing pole

9'–10'
(2.8–3m)
Distance from takeoff pole to fence

In a grid, ground poles such as these assist young horses that become "disunited" after landing or become overzealous in finding their rhythm.

can be approached in canter. "The benefit comes from turning" is one of the guiding principles of training. In a turn, the approach to the fence is prepared. If the beat is interrupted while turning (perhaps by the inside rein acting too strongly) rhythm is interrupted, as well, because the horse's inside leg does not strike sufficiently forward or his muscles tense. However, a faulty beat is not necessarily due to poor rider influence. Apart from health problems (experiencing pain in turning), it may result from poor responsiveness to the aids: the horse resists the lateral bend and tenses up, which is not good preparation for jumping an obstacle. In this case, it helps to do dressage work aimed at lateral bending and follow the principle of "inside leg, outside rein."

Still another kind of fault before the fence is a lack of regularity and rhythm in the canter. It is caused by unsteady contact, in short, a lack of responsiveness to the aids. When checked, the horse refuses to go onto the bit by momentarily putting his forelegs down and/or striking the ground simultaneously with both hind legs. At the same instant, the rider has "no horse in front of him" and tries to drive forward in order to meet the proper takeoff point; then he is forced to check again, and so forth. Beat, rhythm, and impulsion are lost, and it is impossible to jump the fence in a concentrated, relaxed, and precise manner.

It is not only before or after a fence that beat and rhythm are desirable: the demand for movement that is neither rushed nor sluggish may also be carried over to the process of jumping itself. In chapter 4, it will be explained in detail how it is possible for the rider to optimize this process.

All principles of the Training Scale are correlated. To improve one point, the help of the others is needed. However, suppleness is of particular importance.

Suppleness

The goals of invisible communication between horse and rider and the expression of lightness are inextricably linked to suppleness. Sometimes, the term "suppleness" is confused with total relaxedness, but it

▲ *A typical problem for high-spirited or unbalanced horses is they tend to rush their fences. Ground poles in front of and behind the fence may help the horse find his rhythm. A severe response to rushing would only create conflict; overzealousness is better channelled by means of quiet and patient work.*

There is a distinction between *inner* and *outer* suppleness. *Inner* suppleness means the necessary state of mind for an optimum willingness to learn and perform. *Outer* suppleness is the physical precondition for the development of performance.

Inner Suppleness

If a horse is sound, attention must be focused first on his psyche. *There is no outer suppleness without inner suppleness.* Inner suppleness begins long before backing with a basic trust in man. Unfortunately, the ways our sport horses are kept are often shaped by the goals we pursue rather than according to the basic requirements of the original herd and steppe animal. Spookiness, exuberant spirits, overzealousness, or simply a lack of concentration is often a symptom of management that does not comply with the horse's natural requirements. In particular, horses often miss:

● Distinctive social and visual contacts with pals (avoid solitary confinement)
● Free and easy exercise (paddock or pasture time)
● Long, varied, and quiet exercise (phases of relaxation, hacking out)
● Quiet, stress-free handling by rider and groom (horsemanship)
● Individualized diet (or they will "feel their oats")
● A dropped neck and arched back for the major part of the day as were required in the search for food on the steppe

A young horse must from time to time be turned out and allowed to let off steam. A horse that is only allowed exercise when ridden (and always in an obedient manner)

▲ *Ratina Z, one of the most successful horses in the world, in the warm-up area at Aachen, Germany. Despite her being very high-spirited (sometimes "hot"), Ludger Beerbaum occasionally rode her with sharp spurs in order to push her forward when approaching a fence and stop her habit of putting her forelegs down and/or striking the ground simultaneously with both hind legs. He was able to approach the fences more rhythmically and make her take off at a close distance, which she needed because her forward drive tended to flatten her jumping effort.*

means a horse without tension, not a totally relaxed one. The absence of tension applies to the mind as well as the body. There is no true responsiveness to the aids without suppleness.

"Suppleness is the key to success," said Dr. Uwe Schulten-Baumer, ex-show-jumper rider and the most successful dressage trainer of the twentieth century.

In jumping, there are always some horses that, through their successes, defy the necessity of one principle or other of the Training Scale. If lasting success is the aim, suppleness can be neglected least of all.

will never achieve inner suppleness and obedience unless he is tired out. Even at the Cavalry School of Hannover, despite all the military discipline, it was common practice to let the horses run free regularly. In 1940, Major von Busse wrote, "A trick in order to avoid tense and naughty horses: let the young horse under saddle run free in the empty indoor arena for five to ten minutes depending on the time available. You will be surprised how peaceful and relaxed the horse will be after this."[12] (But be careful: in order to avoid injury it is necessary to warm up the horse's circulation by leading the horse first at the walk. Never let a cold horse run around!)

▲ *"Inner suppleness" begins at the stable: with high-spirited horses in particular, the methods of management and exercise should be as near as possible to a horse's natural requirements.*

■ Outer Suppleness

Outer suppleness should be considered the physical condition necessary when performance is demanded. The system as well as the psyche must adjust to the needs of jumping performance; the muscles of a horse with inner tension cannot, or cannot quickly, interact and loosen up, and, tense and cramped muscles cannot develop properly. Although in practice, inner and outer suppleness are worked at simultaneously, only when a horse has achieved inner suppleness can outer suppleness follow.

A certain "working temperature" is also necessary for outer suppleness. This does not only apply to allowing a good blood supply to the muscles, but also providing joints, tendons, and ligaments the preparation time they require before they may be exposed to major strain. And this is not all: the whole Training Scale will only be truly conclusive if the horse is able continuously to alternate between relaxing his muscles and building up "positive body tension" (see p. 56). This body tension demands a forward drive of the horse—the horse should be "in front of the rider's leg."

Each horse has his weak and strong points, so there are differences in suppleness due to type. Some horses seem supple when they have just come out of their stalls, whereas others—the wiry types with short, tense backs—need more time to loosen up. (Horses like this need patient, consistent flatwork daily in order to loosen their muscles.)

At all times, the rider should feel able to let the horse move in a "stretched" outline. Only then can he be sure he is riding a horse that is really responsive to the aids. In the end, it is the same "forward/downward"

---

[12] Roeingh, Rolf (Ed.), *Das deutsche Reiterbuch* (The German rider book), Berlin: Deutscher Archiv-Verlag, 1940.

Working Temperature

Suppleness should not be confused with total relaxation. An easy tensing and relaxing of the muscles can be achieved by different means, depending on the type of horse: lazy horses are woken up and excitable horses are calmed down before they reach a state of optimum receptiveness.

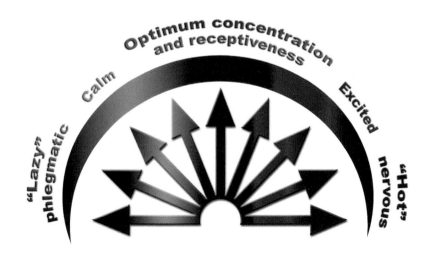

tendency with a relaxed back (essentially *bascule*) that is also desired when jumping.

■ Auxiliary Lessons

By riding turns and bent figures according to the principle "inside leg, outside rein," the horse develops a tendency for stretching downward. If a horse responds to the lightest forward driving aids, flexion and bend may mainly be achieved by weight and leg aids. The inside rein—in combination with the inside leg—is only used to *introduce* the bend. Then the outside rein leads while the bend is maintained by the inside leg driving forward and the outside leg—a hand's width further back—supporting the bend. When the horse wants to stretch forward/downward and the rider is going to allow it, the rider yields the reins and changes to the light seat position, encouraging the horse to swing his back. During this exercise, care should be taken for the hindquarters to remain sufficiently active, or the movements become unbalanced.

■ Suppleness when Jumping

In daily work, suppleness is the first goal to be achieved. It is a basic requirement for a strong-nerved, focused, and content jumper. This makes suppleness the most important principle in the Training Scale for the consistent development of a jumper's potential.

▲ *Encouraging the horse to move with a stretched outline is the key lesson of dressage for jumpers. The horse's back is only able to lift and swing if mind and muscles are relaxed—and the same concept applies when jumping.*

Says Paul Schockemöhle, "If too much pressure is exerted onto a horse, he loses focus on the top rail." And, according to John Whitaker, "Only a relaxed horse is a good horse." The lightweight construction of modern courses ensures that the slightest touch of a rail results in faults; therefore, only suppleness can provide the precision needed to solve the tasks. Modern, careful horses, in particular, are fond of approaching a fence in a comfortable posture (in a loose and relaxed attitude, for example), and when a rider always insists on very close takeoff spots, this may be enough to make very careful horses tense up, negatively affecting their scope.

On the other hand, the heavy Warmblood type is better restrained and "put into a positive body tension" when approaching a fence. These horses (often long and lanky, sometimes even a bit dull when jumping) benefit from a close takeoff point because it requires focus and bascule. By "putting them into tension" a positive strain on mind and muscles is implied; it should not be confused with "tensing them up" (see p. 56).

How do we recognize a lack of suppleness while jumping? Clear symptoms are:

● "Swishing" or clamped tail before and over the fence

● Shying at the ground, spookiness, and poor "opening-up" over fences
● Uneconomical trajectory (jumping too high or landing too far)
● Tense muscles (restrained movement, hollow back)
● Rushing on approach, jumping, or landing
● Landing hard and stiffly
● Breathing not rhythmical, holding breath (breath should match rhythm of canter)
● Ears laid back[13]

So, how do we train the horse to be supple at the jump? Again, the prerequisite is that the horse remains in a receptive frame of mind. Keep environmental conditions as natural as possible and handle the horse in a way that encourages him to trust the people around him. The next goal is outer suppleness (the main characteristic of responsiveness to the aids). Riding over ground poles or cavaletti is integrated into the flatwork and is aimed at lateral bending and developing a stretched outline. In any case, the rider should interfere as little as possible in order to make it easier for the horse to loosen up. When he jumps the horse over a small crossrail, or a bit later through a combination, he is able to limit his aids to a minimum. For a young horse, it is best to approach a fence in a straight line and at the right speed and to

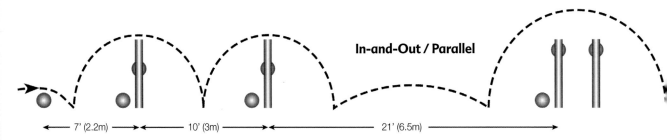

In-and-Out / Parallel

7' (2.2m)   10' (3m)   21' (6.5m)

When the young horse has learned to jump a single fence, a grid consisting of an in-and-out and a parallel may be tackled next. It is a classical exercise for the training of rhythm, suppleness, and technique.

---

[13] When both ears are pinned back, the horse usually feels irritated by the rider's influence. If the horse is naturally a self-assured fighter, such an aggressive expression may just be his style. One ear laid back may also be due to the rider's pronounced influence, but as a general rule this is a sign of a lack of confidence or unhappiness.

meet the point of takeoff at the trot. A more experienced horse may canter over small crossrails. A crossrail has the advantage of naturally guiding the horse to the middle so the rider may again reduce his aids. Jumping small fences is most beneficial for relaxing a horse.

> **With a supple horse, it is easier to make economical use of his power.**

Any future performance is based on a relaxed but attentive mind and muscle interaction that is free of tension.

▲ *Performance can only be developed on a base of complete suppleness. In the warm-up areas of important horse shows you can see how this subject is taken very seriously by the top riders in the world. Here, Calvaro and Willi Melliger jump in a relaxed manner over a small fence. The purpose is loosening up; an energetic takeoff and tucked-up legs is not yet required. First the prerequisite must be right—suppleness.*

Contact

Lightness in a horse is always a result of lightness in the mouth ...

SALOMON DE LA BROUE
(1530–1620)

A light, steady, but elastic connection between the rider's hand and the horse's mouth by means of the reins enables the rider to refine his aids so they are better received and accepted by the horse. This is not only true in flatwork—precise and harmonious riding over a jump course is decisively helped by proper contact, as well. If the reins are too loose, the horse may be frightened when they are taken up again, or he may find himself without guidance in a difficult situation. Too strong a contact is also a disadvantage; if an oversensitive horse is used to constantly yielding to the steady pressure of the bit, he will be upset if the reins become loose in front of a fence, and he will free his head and hollow his back. A less sensitive horse will lean on the bit during his approach, and depending on his temperament, either rush or shift his balance to the forehand and "push himself" too close to the fence for takeoff.

Self-carriage on a light contact is, therefore, essential for the jumper. The rider is obliged to make sure of this. A visible check of self-carriage can be achieved by "giving the reins" for an instant when approaching a fence.

■ Contact and Flexion at the Poll

Contact is a *precondition* of steady flexion at the poll (the horse's head being held so his nose is close to the vertical). With less stable horses, the rider will try to re-establish flexion at the poll between individual fences. It is true, however, that not every horse jumps better when he is flexed at the poll beforehand. Some (especially those with a high percentage of Thoroughbred blood) prefer their heads in a raised and unconstrained position. In particular, clever and naturally rideable horses may be allowed to go around a whole course carrying their heads in a natural position. The rider determines which shape is better suited for a horse so he may develop his full potential. Therefore, the rule is that when jumping a round in a balanced and responsive manner, a horse needs contact, but not always poll flexion.

During the seventies, jumpers were often ridden with their noses behind the vertical. Their necks were so over bent that they seemed to "bite their chests." The following reasons were given: by bringing the horse's back up, suppleness could be facilitated; and responsiveness to the aids and obedience could be improved. This method was practiced excessively, for example, by Alwin Schockemöhle. His outstanding successes on responsive horses seemed to indicate that this striking method was the ideal solution. However, hundreds of followers failed miserably when they tried to imitate his style. By means of running reins, they pulled their horses' heads between their forelegs, but when the reins were taken off the problems were even worse than before.

The following is an excerpt from an interview with Olympic champion Alwin Schockemöhle, approximately twenty-five years after his active career:

At every horse show, horses with running reins were seen. "This is the way Schockemöhle does it," people claimed. It is true. But, they did not realize that I used to ride for about two minutes with my running reins active, and about twenty-eight minutes without them.

The Hannoveraner, 2/74, April, 2002

Putting the horse in a low, overbent position is not necessarily a disadvantage if the horse is on a *light contact* and balanced with engaged hindquarters. But, excessively bending and laterally flexing the neck in this position is often seen used as a check for obedience and responsiveness to the aids. This strict technique always runs the risk of the rider "getting stuck" with the horse because the forward flow of motion beginning with the hind legs and moving over the back is blocked by the over use of the reins. For schooling, this is a dead-end road, and

◀ *Not every jumper has to flex at the poll: Mark Leone riding Legato demonstrates how for a jumper, contact is more important than flexion at the poll.*

▲ *Lajos (ridden by the author) has his nose behind the vertical, but is nevertheless balanced, carries himself, and is obviously loose, responsive, and content. In this case, the position of the nose behind the vertical may be tolerated.*

▲ *The above description does not apply to the flexion at the poll pictured here. Naturally, this horse is higher behind and the extreme flexion of the neck produces a "downhill" tendency. The free carriage of the tail indicates a certain amount of suppleness, but the flow of motion— which should travel forward from the hind legs over a swinging back and back again—is clearly obstructed.*

bending a horse's neck close to his chest seems to me rather like an expression of dominance and an arrogant attitude, as well.

Faults in Contact

Apart from accepting the rein aids, the right kind of contact, which should be sought after by the horse and allowed for by the rider, signifies the horse is contented and that there is an understanding between horse and rider. In jumping, the most serious faults with contact are:

- **Head shaking** This may be caused by the bridle or bit exerting too much pressure or chafing the surrounding tissue, but if we exclude tooth and bitting problems, head shaking is most often caused by constant strong pressure on the tongue and lower jaw. When flexion at the poll is forced by the rider's hands acting backward while the horse is not driven into the bit from behind, the horse may try to evade, disregarding the short-term mouth pain that accompanies throwing his head up in an attempt to rid himself of the permanent pressure. Another possible rider problem is ill-timed taking and giving of the reins so that the rein aids are incomprehensible to the horse.

  It should be mentioned that head shaking is not always caused by the rider; it is occasionally a habitual vice, in which case the symptoms do not occur only when the horse is ridden.

- **Leaning on the bit** A horse leaning on the bit indicates a lack of balance or rideability. It is often connected with a hard mouth. In practice, the horse is pulling, gets deep to the jump, and the rider misses the optimum takeoff point. Grids and combinations at short distances become a problem. Changes in speed and transitions within the gaits may help in this case (see "Collection," p. 62). If, however, the rider tries to solve the problem by exerting even more pressure on the reins, the horse may go from leaning on the bit to pulling. As with head shaking, the horse is willing to disregard harsh, short-term pain in the hope of ridding himself of the annoying pressure of the reins. Of course, such a "dead mouth" may also have genetic reasons. Gerd Wiltfang once made the following remark about the offspring of the stallion Goldlack, "With their mouths they could pull a wheelbarrow out of the muck." Nevertheless, Wiltfang had been very successful with Goldika and Gordon, both by Goldlack and both not exactly "rideable." In this respect, Giulietta with whom my brother won the Grand Prix of Neumünster, was a typical product of her sire, too.

  Quite another cause of a bad mouth is often considered too late: increasing insensitivity of the mouth combined with a shortening of the stride can be the first symptoms of navicular disease.

- **Unilateral tightening** If only one side of the horse is tight or the horse tilts his neck to one side, working on straightness and lateral bending will solve the problem. (This shows how strongly the individual points of the Scale are interlocked and how they have to be regarded as a coherent entity.)

- **Open mouth** Open mouths are seen fairly often shortly before takeoff, especially when half-halts are given with a strong hand because of a very short distance to the fence or because of a lack in responsiveness. It is of vital importance to re-establish a more comfortable contact at least within the last canter stride to ensure a relaxed flight, particularly with young horses (more experienced horses are better able to compensate for such a mistake). Otherwise, this may result in a poor bascule or faults from the hindlegs. An open mouth is usually the result of a dominant rider's hand, or a lack of balance or carrying power—not only when jumping, but also during flatwork. The rider should focus on his horse being able to carry himself. The reins should only be used in combination with the other aids, and only for a short time (as a kind of signal); they should not be abused like a mechanical transmitter of power such as a hand brake.

- **Behind the bit** This problem is frequently seen with "green" horses. If the horse does not seek contact at all, if he "hides behind the bit" as we call it, it is impossible for the rider to maintain his rhythm during the length of a course. The horse is not in front of the leg, and therefore, the rider cannot shorten or lengthen the strides in a precise way. The result is the much dreaded "loose contact" we discussed earlier. In addition, this faulty contact makes it impossible to build up *positive* body tension. Often, a change of bit (to a softer bit made of rubber or leather) will help. And, check the teeth!

- **Tongue over the bit** This fault is usually the consequence of a constant heavy rein influence. Young horses are especially sensitive to this; they try to evade the permanent pressure of the bit, first by pulling their tongues back, then bringing them forward over the bit. This bad habit makes elastic contact impossible, and the horse's responsiveness to the aids worsens. To correct this, first check the rider's influence: is he asking for too much elevation, or too much collection? Are the rein aids given briefly, and are they sufficiently supported by the driving aids so the horse submits to the bit again as quickly as possible? Or, is it a technical problem? Is the bit fitted correctly, creating a wrinkle in the corner of the mouth? If nothing else, a change of bit is recommended.

When then fourteen-year-old, Olympic winner Classic Touch came to Piet Raymakers' stables, he fitted her bit so high that it touched the incisors of her lower jaw. He thought that in this way the high-spirited mare would be more responsive to his rein aids, but he was unable to revive her former successes.

◼ Correcting Problems with Contact

The reason why it is so important for a jumper to stretch deep down with his back swinging in a relaxed way (ideally with his nose close to the vertical) is that he will only be able to develop his full jumping potential if he is supple and does not tighten his back. However, the forward/downward posture should not be used exclusively in flatwork (with the exception of a horse with an unstable back). With a short distance or grid, a certain elevation is required without any resistance to the rider's hands. Therefore, daily flatwork must be a permanent interplay between an elevated and a stretched outline, between collection and extension, between effort and relaxation.

It is not necessarily harmful to bend the horse's neck behind the vertical or flex his neck sideways in an exaggerated way, as long as the rider succeeds in keeping the hindquarters engaged, thus maintaining balance and self-carriage of his mount. But, how few riders are really able to influence the hind legs without neglecting to yielding the reins in time! Without the increased engagement of the hindquarters, the deep position of the neck results in tense muscles or a "tough" mouth. Then, the only remedy is for the rider to take one step back and revisit basic dressage work.

Most problems with contact are caused by poor obedience to the leg aids, which leads to unengaged hindquarters, preventing the horse from balancing himself, and in the end, carrying himself. What does this mean? If the horse appears to maintain the posture demanded by the rider by his own free will, we speak of self-carriage. This should not be confused with being "behind the bit" because the horse should go into the bit regardless of the posture demanded by the rider. Contact should always exist, but it should be soft. The Greek philosopher Xenophon already knew, "...if a horse feels irritated, he will show tense paces; but if you yield the reins after sharpening him up, he will carry himself with a noble attitude because with soft reins he feels free of the bit."[14] This means "engage the hindquarters (drive the horse forward into the bit) and release the flow of motion over the horse's back to the front."

François Robichon de la Guérinière (1688—1751) called the act of encouraging self-carriage through the application of short half-halts followed by a giving of the reins: *descente de main* (descent of hand).

"Descente de main" is an excellent means of calming a horse and activating his mouth, as well as overcoming certain difficulties with the mouth. Even the smallest irritation in the horse's mouth can result in his jaw stiffening; harmony is usually restored immediately if the rider gives the reins—the horse will instantly yield and champ the bit. The essential point is that the horse does not in the least change his head carriage or speed…Care should be taken to ensure that the reins are not yielded or the "descente de main" is not executed if the horse is on the forehand; both must be performed after a half-halt and at the moment when the rider feels the hind legs bending and coming forward. Then he should carefully yield the reins or perform the "descente de main." The difficulty of finding the exact moment to do this makes this aid one of the finest and most useful in equitation… if contact is interrupted the very moment when the horse bends and lifts his hind legs forward, he will inevitably become light in the rider's hand because there is no support left for his head.

The horse's obedience to the leg aids is the basis of any contact correction. In order

---

[14] Mayer, Anton, *Das Reiterbuch* (The rider book), Wiesbaden: Rheinische Verlags Anstalt GmbH (p. 35).

to check or improve obedience to the leg aids, practice leg-yielding head-to-the-wall. The wall or fence of the arena helps limit necessary rein influence, and a young horse with a strong forward drive or a horse that needs to improve his receptiveness to the leg aids will happily perform the lesson far more quickly.

With more advanced horses, obedience to the leg aids is improved by picking up a canter from the walk, trotting from a halt, extensions, and lateral work. The point of the work is to encourage the horse to respond to the slightest of leg aids. Some problems with the horse's mouth are actually solved in this way; impulsion is developed and the horse may be "driven into the bit."

Other valuable lessons for improving contact via lateral work are bent figures ridden with a dominant inside leg and leading outside rein (up to shoulder-in on a circle[15]). This is an excellent means for developing a stretched outline, especially with horses with a tense back, as suppleness has a positive influence on contact.

Jumping a Horse "Into the Bit"

Contact in front of and over the jump—especially in combinations and grids—provides lead, support, and security for a young horse. It is of outstanding importance in the training of jumpers because it helps avoid many a misunderstanding and irritation between horse and rider.

By maintaining his aids, the expert rider is able to jump the horse, not only with contact, but also with flexion at the poll. This is "jumping a horse into the bit." It is mostly used in training and in order to improve responsiveness to the aids (see "Collection," p. 62), but it may also be applied to certain situations when riding a course, such as to prepare the horse for restraining or turning rein aids that follow an obstacle. Then these do not come as a surprise to the horse when the reins are taken up after the jump, and he may prepare himself for the task to come. With a certain type of horse (one that does not naturally make full use of his body or become disunited while jumping) this aid occasionally improves the jumping process or helps keep the horse in balance.

In jumping as well as in dressage it is important "to go with the horse." Using the reins without simultaneously and correspondingly using the legs does not have the desired effect; the insensitive horse leans on the bit even more, while the sensitive horse

▲ *Jumping the horse "into the bit." Such a marked "framing-in" of the horse is seldom seen in jumping. The purpose is to keep the horse collected over the fence, quicken takeoff without flattening the trajectory, or prepare for a close turn. Without dominant driving aids, though, this much flexion at the poll would affect impulsion and/or bascule over the fence.*

---

[15] It is interesting to note that this lesson improves virtually all principles of the Training Scale.

feels punished and loses his bascule. Moreover, this "reins only" technique only makes sense in connection with a deep takeoff point because its purpose is to transform the horse's trajectory into an "upright semi-oval." A long takeoff point requires the horse to stretch himself, and flexion at the poll would counteract this natural movement.

■ Positive Body Tension

A jumper has to be encouraged to accept a contact and develop a self-carriage that enables the rider to ride him at all times in a light and supple way or in a certain state of "tension." I like to call this kind of tension within the horse's body "positive body tension" because it should not be confused with collection or with "tensing up."

Positive body tension is a consequence of the rider driving the horse "into his hand" with constant restraining rein aids. A rider on a horse with the appropriate body tension should feel he is being "pulled" toward the fence by the horse. In this way, the rider is able to give the horse more confidence (in front of awe-inspiring obstacles, for example). Some horses also benefit from positive body tension in order to quicken at takeoff or "open up" (see "Total Process," p. 87), so for spreads, too, it is usually indispensable.

In order to prevent the horse from getting too strong over the length of a course, he should be well trained so that a few half-halts are enough to remove all body tension. Self-carriage is achieved by simultaneously connecting even the slightest rein aid with the driving aids, immediately followed by a yielding of the reins. When this process is repeated at regular intervals according to the rhythm of movements, the horse has no opportunity to lean on the bit. There are,

however, two exceptions: with very experienced horses, the aids are no longer necessary, and very young horses may be confused by this combination of aids within the half-halt. A horse that has just been backed will not understand the interaction of rein and leg aids because early in his training, his pace is slowed by gently applying the rein aid alone. A schooled and experienced horse, however, has learned to balance himself after a half-halt and will often automatically step under his center of gravity without leaning on the bit.

If a jumper is to jump in a balanced and supple manner, self-carriage is of utmost importance.

Impulsion

A human high jumper improves his results by approaching the bar with elastic and springy motions; for the jumping horse, impulsion is of similar importance. The term "impulsion" is—in dressage as well as in jumping—often confused with increased speed by beginners. As Colonel Alois Podhajsky aptly remarked, "Most riders believe that it is impulsion when they hear the wind whistling in their ears. As a matter of fact, real impulsion only becomes evident in collection."

■ Disposition and Training

There are horses that naturally move with a lot of impulsion. The type of impulsion that is important for responsiveness to the aids, however, must be trained, not bred. This thesis is emphasized by another look toward the realm of competitive dressage. I quote Christian Pläge:

Young horses that are born with exaggerated trotting steps are later on often found to have difficulty when increased collection is required. They are unable to vary their long strides and at the same time retain rhythm, suppleness, and impulsion. By means of their enormous propulsive forces, the motion seems very dynamic, but these horses find it hard to transform propulsive force into true carrying power.[16]

This sort of impulsion in cantering and jumping pits the motion of the horse against the rider, who is not able to "go with the horse" and yield the reins—essential for suppleness. Either the horse gets too close to the fence or he takes off sooner than intended.

On the other hand, impulsion achieved by schooling is distinguished by the hocks bending more and the hind legs swinging further forward. It has nothing to do with tense leg actions where the limbs swing backward and upward like a chicken on the run. Only a supple and active back allows for the hind legs to swing forward, thus providing the precondition for true collection and, finally, for responsiveness to the aids.

How is this kind of impulsion achieved in jumpers? To begin with, everything that is suited to activating the hind legs and making the back swing will help. Key lessons are canter-trot-canter transitions, changes of speed at the trot and canter, as well as shoulder-in. For collected work, it is essential that collection is always followed by extension of the pace. This makes it easier to maintain or improve impulsion (plus the "from-behind-toward-the-front" tendency and the rider's ability to "go with the horse") when the steps or strides are shortened and collected again.

■ Impulsion, not Cadence

In trot and canter impulsion, you can recognize a visible moment of suspension. Do not confuse this kind of impulsion with "cadence." In competitive dressage cadenced paces (for instance, a prolonged moment of suspension) are desirable because this elongation gives the horse a prouder expression. In dressage for jumpers, this is not desirable because it would make the horse's movements uneconomical. To exaggerate responsiveness to the aids a little bit, in competitive dressage it serves beauty, while in dressage for jumpers, it serves to ride a round fast and without faults.

Some young horses are not yet able to control their impulsion while jumping, but experience and increased responsiveness to the aids allow the trajectory of their jumps to be influenced by the rider.

Green horse

Supple and experienced horse

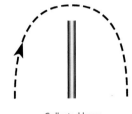

Collected horse

---

[16] Pläge, Christian, *Den richtigen Draht finden* (Finding the right connection), Mainz: Fachverlag Fraund, Mainz, 1995 (p. 71).

Toward the Fence with Impulsion

Cantering with impulsion enables the rider to wait longer before jumping. Regardless of the situation, a proper distance may almost always be reached from an elastic canter stride. If this impulsion is lacking in his approach, the inexperienced rider will tend to increase his driving aids in a way that only serves to disunite the horse. The trainer is then often heard to cry out, "More speed!" although "More impulsion!" would be the more suitable correction. Impulsion is needed to "compress" a horse and enable him to take off fluently and fly willingly over the fence. If basic speed is increased, this only causes the distances to get shorter, which in turn again affects the flow of motion.

A too short takeoff point affects the development of impulsion while jumping, especially in a young horse with a "big engine" that is not yet sufficiently schooled for collection. The horse is likely to fear touching the front rail and so will hesitate before taking off. This is why at this stage of a young horse's training, grids and combinations with proper distances are preferred. If a ridden distance is not quite right, it can be compensated for by riding the horse forward. Impulsion may also be developed by positioning ground lines further away from fences in order to make it easier for the horse to see the distances. (Triple bars or parallels can work if their first rails are slightly lowered.) Increasing speed after landing may also serve to improve impulsion for the following jumps.

Jumping with Impulsion

For a jumper, impulsion also means that he "pulls through" or "finishes" his jump. This aptly describes why impulsion must not be interrupted during the jump process. The horse needs to move with impulsion not only when approaching a fence, but also when taking off, in the air, and in his landing, because only by courageously transforming impulsion into an upward and forward motion can he develop *scope*. However, this impulsion while jumping is only valuable to the rider if it is produced by him, for only then can he control it at all times.

When my brother Alois had won several advanced competitions riding Aperio, his top horse at the time, Power Light, fell ill. So, it was time to start Aperio in his first Grand Prix competitions. Now a problem, which had been noticed for some time but had not mattered much as long as the requirements were not too challenging, became an issue: in combinations, especially when they ended with a spread, Aperio lost impulsion. He gave his rider a feeling of scope when jumping a single parallel, but when jumping a double or triple combination, he broke off over the final fence and slid over the last rail on his belly—he would not fly.

This problem could not be solved with stronger leg aids during the takeoff. (From early on, Aperio had only responded to increased driving aids with a steeper, rather than longer, trajectory.) So, we practiced over a high combination. This was not unusual, but this time, impulsion was demanded not from above by the rider, but from the ground by an assistant with a long whip. And, believe it or not, after the whip had been strategically flicked twice, Aperio sud-

denly understood what it was all about. He pulled through! Once and for all, it dawned on him that jumping was much easier if he maintained impulsion in combinations, as well.

Again and again it becomes evident that all points of the Training Scale are interconnected. For instance, *impulsion* is based on *suppleness*: the supple play of the muscles, which tense and relax in turn. Suppleness is encouraged by a regular and diligent *rhythm* in motion. Rhythm also indicates whether the impulsion we produce is the right one, for impulsion that implies faulty rhythm cannot be supple and cannot lead to responsiveness to the aids. Suppleness, rhythm, and impulsion can only be achieved if the *contact* is correct, and only a *straight* horse will move on both hands with the right contact. Changes of speed are the measure of choice for producing impulsion, and they require *collection,* which cannot be achieved if the horse is not straight.

Straightness

Impulsion and straightness are interlinked. When jumping, we want a horse with a powerful takeoff and a lot of scope. It is with straightness that the forces are combined, as only when straightened can a horse place his hind legs exactly under his center of gravity.

Very few horses naturally move on one track with both their fore- and hind legs. Straightness is the base for bringing the rider/horse combination into mutual balance, and taking schooling as a whole, straightness is the prerequisite for collection (stepping closer to the center of gravity). "A horse is straight if he is equally supple on both sides, and the hind legs always follow the track of the forelegs on straight lines, as well as on circles."[17] Only when both sides of the horse are symmetrically stretched and strengthened can he develop his full potential.

◼ Useful Dressage Exercises

To achieve straightness, the gymnastic effects of lateral bending can be valuable. The principle of "inside leg—outside rein" is the guideline for this work. One very useful lesson for straightening is shoulder-in. Dr. Reiner Klimke, one time the world's most successful dressage rider, remarked:

Shoulder-in is a valuable schooling lesson because by applying diagonal aids, the rider is able to improve the straightness of his horse. Diagonal aids mean that the horse is pushed by the inside leg toward the supporting outside rein, thus becoming straight through his longitudinal axis.[18]

Bending is not the only helpful lesson. Regrettably, the straightening effect of a correct counter-canter is often neglected in a jumper's flatwork.

Even if a horse has more problems on one side than on the other, care should be taken to do the same amount of work on both. For one thing, the "sweet side" of the horse (as it is sometimes called) gives the rider more opportunity to reward the horse, which encourages the horse to cooperate; for another, it will ensure symmetrical muscle development and suppleness.

Many books on the subject, such as *Advanced Techniques of Dressage (Richtlinien für Reiten und Fahren)* [Kenilworth Press, UK / Half Halt Press, US] explain how poor lat-

[17] Müseler, Wilhelm, *Riding Logic*, London: Methuen & Co., 1966.
[18] Klimke, Reiner, and Werner Ernst, *Klimke on Dressage*, Boonsboro, MD: Half-Halt Press, 1992.

eral bending is due to shortened muscles on the "hollow" side of the horse. If a horse is tight on his left side, the muscles on his right side need to be stretched with suitable exercises. If a horse is able to scratch his head with both the right and the left hind foot, and yet resists the slightest attempt to bend him, the cause must be looked for elsewhere. As Kurt Albrecht, former director of the Spanish Riding School of Vienna, put it, "Almost any kind of problem in a horse can be traced back to a lack of schooling of the hindquarters."[19] This holds true in this case. The starting point is obedience to the leg aids. Only when the horse's corresponding hind leg moves forward, or forward and sideways in answer to light leg pressure, can the rider "bend the horse around his inside leg." In daily routine, most problems with lateral bending or contact are solved by merely applying the aids in a more skillful way.

▉ Straightening before Jumping

Young horses often show a tendency toward a certain side when jumping. This makes straightening part of jump training, the necessity of which is emphasized by the following points:

- Young horses run out more easily if they do not approach the fence in a straight line. They fall out over their outside shoulder.
- A balanced canter (and consequently, a good jump) is impossible if the hind legs move to one side or the other of the center of gravity. And, as a rule, a horse that is balanced when taking-off (instead of on his forehand) is quicker in lifting his forelegs.
- When a horse jumps a fence at an angle,

not all his power is transferred into the forward and upward motion but is lost sideways instead.
- When jumping a considerable spread, jumping at an angle makes the fence even wider and uses up energy unnecessarily.
- In a triple combination, for example, it is very unpleasant if the horse's sideways tendency takes you closer and closer to the standards with each jump, or even ends in a run-out.
- The degree of difficulty of a related distance in a bend or turn is changed if the horse does not follow the ideal line.
- When a horse swerves to the wrong side while approaching a jump, it can cost valuable tenths of seconds.
- Only a rider whose horse does not drift to the outside can attempt a very short turn toward the next jump.
- If a horse swerves to the inside while turning, a distance, which before had been correct, may now be found to be too short.

How can we avoid this drifting, swerving, and jumping at angles? Firstly, the straighter the horse is in his flatwork, the straighter he'll be on the jump course.

Every jump begins with the approach out of a turn, and the turn must first be completed before you can deal with the jump. A rider who allows his horse's shoulder to fall out during a turn should not be surprised if the horse jumps the fence at an angle or runs out. A straight jump begins with a straight approach. As in dressage, the diagonal aids align the forehand to the track of the hindquarters.

Once the horse has left the ground, the direction can only be influenced by weight

---

[19] Albrecht, Kurt, *Ausbildungshilfen für Pferd und Reiter* (Training aids for horse and rider), BLV München, 1992 (pp. 96—97).

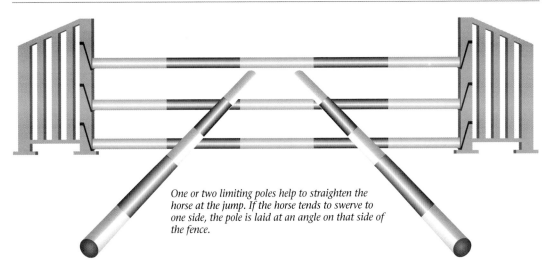

One or two limiting poles help to straighten the horse at the jump. If the horse tends to swerve to one side, the pole is laid at an angle on that side of the fence.

and leg aids. A rider trying to correct the direction by means of the inner rein will only endanger the bascule without solving the real problem. Also, in this case the principle, "Pulling at the inside rein drives you to the outside" applies. When the rider pulls at the inside rein, the horse is free to evade over his outside shoulder.

So, for example, if the horse tends to go to the left while jumping, then the rider should put more weight into his right stirrup during the takeoff and the flight. Driving aids are provided by the left leg positioned slightly back. (The same aids signal the desired lead after landing.) When a horse drifts to one side while approaching a jump, the reasons may be as follows:

● A lack of a leading outside rein
● A lack of responsiveness to the aids
● The horse has not been sufficiently straightened by flatwork

Jumping at an angle may also develop as a result of poor training. If a young horse that is not yet able to collect himself for takeoff is consistently ridden too close to a fence, he may be encouraged to jump at an angle. Because he wants to avoid making a mistake, he tries to avoid the first rail by swerving slightly to one side. To be able to "put himself together" would require a higher degree of collection than he can master at this stage.

From the very first training session, an experienced rider tries to straighten the horse at the jump. Jumping small crossrails already encourage a horse to look for the middle of the fence. The rider will always take care to continue deliberately in a straight line after landing. This is essential—especially with a young horse. By allowing the horse to turn, the rider involuntarily encourages him to jump at an angle.

Of course, a horse may also be straightened by riding turns in a conscious way. For instance, if a horse shows a tendency to jump to the left side, the rider consciously rides a right turn several times after the jump. This may be checked by jumping a fence that is only about 6' 6" (2m) wide between the standards. Moreover, this task is useful because narrow fences may be part of course, even at the lower levels.

Collection

For straightness, lessons in collection are required—again underlining the fact that no point of the Training Scale may dispense with any other. The "father of French equitation," Antoine Pluvinel, discovered the connections between rhythm, collection, and responsiveness to the aids long before the Scale had been developed.

> *This lesson (collection), performed in the right way, makes the horse light and elevates him, places him on his hindquarters and pushes him together; it makes him accept the hand and leg aids willingly. This enables him to perform the required exercises better and eases the whole matter considerably.*
>
> ANTOINE PLUVINEL
> *(1555–1620)*

▪ Does a Jumper Need to Be Collected?

Is it really true that a jumper needs work in collection in order to jump well? Occasionally you hear, "But a good rider can compensate for a lack of collection with forward!" As a matter of fact, time and again, there were top riders who were able to overcome their horses' blatant weaknesses in this regard with skillful riding. Today, though, courses have become technically more demanding and require a well trained horse. The following arguments should further emphasize the value of collected work for the jumper:

● Fundamentally, the development of the carrying force assists in keeping a sport horse healthy.[20] Even without a rider the horse naturally carries 57 percent of his weight on his forehand. If the hindquarters of a jumper are not encouraged in flatwork to assume more weight, early wear and tear of the forehand may be the consequence. By using suppling and strengthening

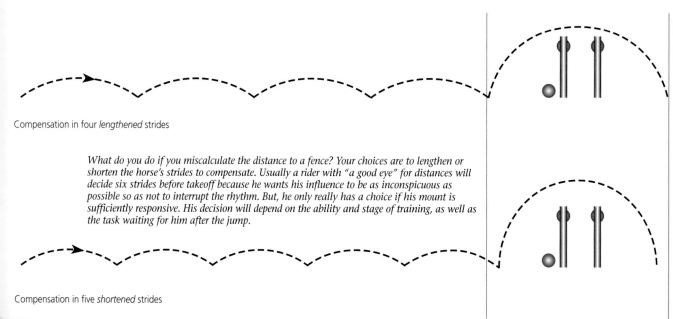

Compensation in four *lengthened* strides

What do you do if you miscalculate the distance to a fence? Your choices are to lengthen or shorten the horse's strides to compensate. Usually a rider with "a good eye" for distances will decide six strides before takeoff because he wants his influence to be as inconspicuous as possible so as not to interrupt the rhythm. But, he only really has a choice if his mount is sufficiently responsive. His decision will depend on the ability and stage of training, as well as the task waiting for him after the jump.

Compensation in five *shortened* strides

---

[20] See Steinbrecht, Gustav, *The Gymnasium of the Horse*, Xenophon Press, 1995.

exercises, you can reduce the number of conditioning jumps (along with their inherent weight-shift to the forehand) needed in training.

● Lessons in collecting improve control in between fences. In young horse divisions, many a distance may be attempted by increased forward driving or by the horse inserting a short canter stride. At this stage, rhythm is still more important than correct point of takeoff. At more advanced levels of competition, however, more precision is required in the approach because of the height of the fence. Occasionally, it may be necessary to shorten the strides. To give a typical example: from a distance of four canter strides out, a rider realizes he will miss the ideal takeoff point by 6 feet, and he knows from experience that by compensating with a longer stride he will meet with less resistance from his horse (whose carrying force has not yet been fully developed); so, the rider *lengthens* each stride by approximately 1½ feet.

But, if he is jumping into a tight distance or combination, *lengthening* the strides will only transfer the problem to the next jump. When strides are lengthened in such a way, there is the risk that the horse will become either too big or flat at the following jump. In this scenario, a well schooled jumper allows the rider to insert a fifth stride by *shortening* each stride—the more elegant solution as it enables the rider to "keep his horse together." This remedy is only possible if impulsion has not been neglected in collected work. Only the "bounce" that comes from collection will give the rider

enough security to "wait and see" before actually jumping. Out of such a canter, he will sense he is able to develop a powerful jump at any given moment.

● In competitive show jumping, unrelated distances and combinations have to be expected (see "Combinations and 'Distances,'" p. 94). Helena Weinberg says:

> *When a horse is six, you reach the point when you will have to cope with difficult distances, when you will have to start "riding backward." In the young horse divisions, courses are designed to make horses go forward. What is asked for is always a forward canter, a forward compensation. This is wonderful for a four- or five-year-old, but at the age of six the horses have to allow themselves to be shortened or collected at times.*
>
> The Hannoveraner, 7/76, August, 2002

A well trained horse should even allow his rider to shorten his stride at the last element of a triple combination.

● Collection may influence the process of jumping. Out of a collected, self-carried canter, longer or "downhill" horses, in particular, will find it easier to stay balanced at the jump. They no longer "push into" the fence, and more space remains in front of the first rail. Over a vertical, the trajectory reaches its summit over the highest rail (with young, still unbalanced horses it usually lies a bit further back) when the hind legs stride closer to the center of gravity. This training will improve and secure the technique of the forelegs with those horses that are careful but do not naturally tuck up their forelegs in an ideal manner.[21] Faults by the hind legs are also often rooted in the same problem (see "Hind Leg Technique," p. 84).

● In competitions against the clock, better maneuverability often makes the difference between winning and losing. Let us assume that in the jump-off there is a long run to a vertical, followed by a change of direction by 180 degrees. Without well-developed carrying power, the horse will not be able to approach the vertical at full speed because this would make the trajectory too long and too flat with the associated risk of a fault. In addition, after landing, another stride will have to be added before the turn. This would take twice as long. A trained horse ready to be collected can be ridden toward the jump at high speed. The rider is able to shorten the last few strides and transform the trajectory from a semicircle to a semi-oval shape. He can then begin the turn as early as above the fence.

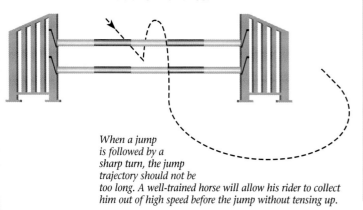

When a jump is followed by a sharp turn, the jump trajectory should not be too long. A well-trained horse will allow his rider to collect him out of high speed before the jump without tensing up.

[21] See Morris, George, *The American Jumping Style*, New York: Doubleday, 1993.

▓ How Is Collection Achieved?

Don't you ever forget that (forward) motion is the heart and soul of equitation and it is initiated by the hindquarters of the horse.

LUDWIG SEEGER
(1794–1865)

Now then, how is this readiness for collection achieved with a jumper? And what degree of collection is necessary for show jumping?

Let us start with preparation in flatwork. Before we try to train to reduce speed on a straight line, there are some other exercises to gently introduce the horse to collection. Picking up the canter from the walk requires carrying power and can be ridden long before the first canter-walk transition. In addition, transition exercises within the energetic gaits of trot and canter, for instance, half-halts from the canter to the trot, are very valuable when ridden in more of an "uphill" position.

Some riders feel that a horse needs only to learn to maintain the canter and that transitions are unnecessary. But, trot-canter-trot transitions, if well performed, do not encourage the horse to fall out of the canter. In fact, the horse learns to activate his hindquarters and remain supple in the back while at the same time rebalancing himself. With a loose and supple horse, any half-halt is transmitted from the active mouth via a supple back to the hindquarters. A fluently and diligently performed downward transition, in balance, indicates that the half-halt was successful. This is to say that correctly performed full halts and half-halts are the foundation of any kind of increased collec-

▲ *The suppling effect of lateral bending is not only noticeable longitudinally. Diagonal aids help to align the hindquarters with the forehand. If lateral bending is achieved by the horse bending around the rider's inside leg rather than mainly inside rein, then the horse's inside hind leg is able to take a long swing forward, as demonstrated here. Thus, the horse is also balanced in his transverse axis (see p. 71).*

tion, the basis of any shortening of stride before the jump.

Half pirouettes and turns on the haunches encourage collection, as do as sharp turns during course riding. As described before in "Straightness" (see p. 59), a precise approach to a fence depends on a successful turn beforehand. The horse should not fall out "over his shoulder" or into the trot; he should remain balanced and willingly accept lateral bending.

Besides their gymnastic effect, lateral bending exercises are also useful for collecting the horse. The carrying forces are gradually improved by riding voltes and serpentines, and by increasing and decreasing the width of a circle. Especially in the volte, the horse's inside hind leg is encouraged to

assume weight; the rider is able to use his driving aids while at the same time reducing speed.

Shoulder-in is another valuable exercise for introducing a young horse to collection. By concentrating on his inside hind leg he will more easily understand what collection is all about, as compared to working on a straight line. Shoulder-in is also recommended for horses that tend to rush their fences, get out of control, or shift their weight to their forehand. Approaching small fences in the shoulder-fore or shoulder-in position teaches them to stay in balance instead of "shooting off."

Note: when the shoulder is limited by the outside rein and bending is achieved by the inside leg (which also keeps the horse's hind leg active) a yielding inside rein releases forward motion. These aids do not only promote collection, but in a jumping course help keep the horse "on his legs." Slipping and falling in turns (especially when the ground is slippery) is generally caused by the inside rein being pulled.

▮ Applying Aids for Collection

The fourth phase of a canter stride ends in a nodding movement: the horse's head and neck work up momentum for the last phase of suspension. If this rolling motion is interrupted by half-halts given at the wrong moment or a rider's unyielding hands, resistance to the bit is the consequence and no carrying force is developed. Applying driving aids at the moment of takeoff, or interference via the reins during the nodding movement, provides nothing but resistance. If, on the other hand, the uphill motion triggered by each stride is briefly supported and increased, and the rolling motion allowed for, collection is achieved but not at the expense of suppleness and balance. In other

words, the collecting aids should use the *natural* movements of the horse. At the canter, the aids for collection are most effective shortly before the phase of suspension. Half-halts should be given at the end of the rolling motion between the fourth and fifth phase when the hind leg swings forward and the horse moves upward again.

▮ Jump Exercises to Increase Collection

● **Volte before and after the jump** If a volte at the canter no longer offers a problem in flatwork, it can be included in a small jump. This helps prevent the horse from becoming disunited before and after the jump; instead, he becomes more balanced. In addition, he grows accustomed to the aids for sharp turns before and after a fence (see "Jumping Against the Clock," p. 101). As an alternative, three cavaletti may be laid on a circle line at a maximum distance of 10 feet (3m). For both exercises, the horse should be flexed at the poll and bent laterally. This kind of lateral bending—and similar exercises—not only straighten and supple the horse, but also "put him together."

● **Half-halts, full halts, and rein-back**
Responsiveness to the aids at a jump can also be improved by the following exercise: before, after, or between fences reduce speed; then, perform a full halt, and—if the horse's stage of development allows—initiate four to six steps of rein-back before striking off again at the canter. The full halt before and/or after the jump improves the horse's balance and teaches him to remain responsive. It is essential not to work

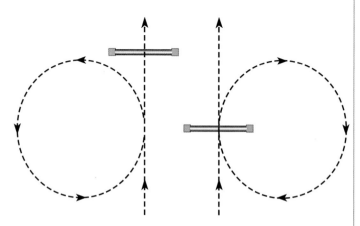

A volte in front of the jump improves responsiveness to the aids during the last few strides before takeoff. Adding a volte that begins on landing and includes the jump helps the rider straighten and collect the horse.

"against the horse," especially for the full halt after the jump. The horse must be allowed to develop his own ideas about what is required from him. He should not feel provoked to run from the strong influence. This is the only way the rider will succeed in teaching the horse not to become disunited at the next jump.

Performing a rein-back after the halt checks the horse's responsiveness to the aids and, in addition, increases the collecting effect of the full halt. When the transitions are not yet satisfactory, a calmly performed rein-back after the halt sometimes works wonders. In my experience, the horse will stay much better balanced in halts that follow. The rein-back may be considered successful if the horse steps back willingly in a fluent motion.

● Approaching the fence in shoulder-in

This is an interesting exercise that improves self-carriage, rhythm, and balance. In preparation, the horse approaches a single ground pole in shoulder-fore or shoulder-in, then a small crossrail is added. During the turn toward the jump, a volte is inserted—from which the shoulder-in is developed. It is essential to maintain the flexion for shoulder-in up

▲ *Approaching a fence in the shoulder-fore or shoulder-in is an excellent exercise to improve rhythm, self-carriage, and balance during the last few strides in front of a fence. The fence does not need to be as high as pictured here; a ground pole is sufficient for initial training.*

to the very point of takeoff.

Rhythmic canter strides are encouraged when a ground pole is laid on the ground at a distance of up to 16' 6" (5m) before, and 10' (3m) after the fence. This helps transform the jump trajectory from

This exercise is aimed at increasing collection in front of a jump. If the horse has difficulty remaining balanced during the last canter stride, a volte may be ridden in front of the ground pole or the fence may be built a short distance from the short side of the arena and jumped out of the corner (each corner is a quarter-volte). Ideally, the horse should stride just over the first ground pole so as to leave enough space for the jump.

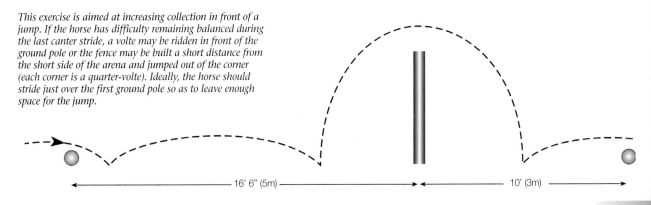

|← 16' 6" (5m) →|← 10' (3m) →|

a semicircle to a semi-oval shape. With young horses, it is recommended to approach the first canter pole coming from a turn (quarter volte) or a volte in order to attain the degree of collection necessary for this distance.

◼ Beware of "Too Much, Too Soon"

Collecting a horse in front of a jump is not meant to suppress the horse's keenness. He should always be allowed to pull a bit toward the fence. But, ambition on his part should not necessarily be connected with a loss of balance. Moreover, his canter stride must remain under control at all times.

The rider should not try to improve control at the cost of rhythm or suppleness. For example, in principle, it is true that frequent transitions improve suppleness, but it is a good idea to insert longer periods of trotting or cantering at an even pace from time to time. Equally, the horse should not be surprised by the aids when the rider asks for changes of speed within a gait. If the rider does not succeed in developing a rhythmical canter during training, finding the optimum approach to a fence remains a mere matter of luck.

A high degree of collection should not be expected to be achieved quickly. It needs years to develop; otherwise, there is the risk of the horse being overtaxed by the new, and at first, unaccustomed strain. He must be conditioned in small steps because this stage of schooling puts stress on the back and hindquarters in a way he has not been used to.[22]

Care should not only be taken where physical aspects are concerned. This kind of work is very strenuous and, therefore, should always be alternated with relaxing exercises in order to avoid the horse becoming mentally taxed (as when riding jump courses—states of tension and relaxation should alternate consistently). The horse should be happy with his work because only a happy and mentally balanced jumper will develop to his full potential.

Responsiveness to the Aids

Problems must be solved by allowing the horse's muscles sufficient time to gain strength. The gymnastic exercises necessary for suppleness, balance, obedience, and collection should not be neglected. Without these exercises, no horse will show free and easy movements... regardless of the task the horse is trained for, be it fox hunting, jumping, the performance of difficult school figures, or all these tasks together.

FRANÇOIS ROBICHON DE LA GUÉRINIÈRE
(1688–1751)

Responsiveness to the aids means that all aids are willingly accepted and unconstrained harmony between horse and rider exists. This should not be confused with forcing and dominating a horse. When training begins, the rider's "hierarchical" position should be generally accepted by the horse, but originating from this, a partnership with equal rights should develop.

Ease of manner is a fundamental distinguishing feature of responsiveness to the aids. With regard to this, Helena Weinberg remarks:

The most important thing when jumping a course is the attitude of the horse. He has to contribute by thinking

---

[22] Müseler, Wilhelm, *Riding Logic*, London: Methuen & Co., 1966.

Walzerkönig ridden by Franke Sloothaak was much admired during the 1980s. He was a perfect example of a horse that matured into a world class jumper when his responsiveness was improved. His former rider had considered him only a puissance horse—though of some scope—because originally, he lacked that ultimate quality: the instinct for recognizing dangerous situations early and avoiding faults by thinking for himself. Thus, Sloothaak had to be able to control every inch; his half-halts had to be willingly accepted so that even in a one-stride combination, he would be able to "keep his horse away from the rail." Originally, the horse hadn't been very rideable, practical, or smart either, but thanks to his scope, his willingness, and gymnastic dressage, he finally became one of the few horses able (at least sometimes) to beat Milton, the horse of the century.

▲ *Franke Sloothaak demonstrates what a perfectly balanced horse should look like. Out of an "uphill" canter like this—on the bit, with the slightest of connections to the rider's hand—jumping is made easy for the horse.*

for himself and striving for success along with his rider. I leave my horses a lot of their own character. I do not dominate them but try to make them side with me. I am 5' 3" (1.6m) tall, and I cannot force a horse to do anything—it would not work! In the long run, force does not get you anywhere.

The Hannoveraner, 7/76, August, 2002

Dressage should have nothing in common with "drilling" a horse to do something. The goal is to use control in order to be able to ride forward according to the principle, "Gain freedom through submission, and forward riding through responsiveness to the aids!" Rhythmical extensions, collection, full and half-halts, and the rein-back are the touchstones of responsiveness to the aids; this applies to dressage for jumpers as well as competitive dressage. Only when the rider is able to approach any fence out of any situation without visible aids can the horse be considered truly responsive. With such a horse, it is possible to jump a course with more precision and more scope.

A rider who embraces the effort and strain of competition, either as an amateur or as a professional, logically wants to succeed. This success need not necessarily take the form of a blue ribbon; any trainer knows the wonderful feeling of getting the best performance from a horse or preparing a horse for major tasks and riding successful

▲ *"The benefit lies in turning": Aperio is bent around the inside leg and thus able to see the next task in time. His poll is the highest point, his nose is close to the vertical, and contact is as desired. The hind leg swinging far forward indicates good balance. His focused look and freely carried tail indicate suppleness and he is looking forward to jumping the next fence.*

rounds, even if he does not win. Success in jumping depends strongly on responsiveness to the aids. The less rideable a jumper is, the more decisive the rider's responses must be, and the more the pair's success will depend on luck.

■ Three Axes of Balance

As I've explained, the horse's willing acceptance of the aids is improved by flatwork. In order to execute tasks in an easy and unconstrained manner, balance is needed. As a result of the excellent qualities bred into jumpers today, fewer and fewer horses are born with serious problems balancing themselves. Nevertheless, balance remains a fundamental aspect of schooling. Imagine three axes to which the jumper must be aligned: first there are the *longitudinal* (straightness) and the *transverse* axes (collection). Although collecting exercises are used for straightening the horse, straightness is a crucial principle and has priority over collection. Only a straight horse that has been equally developed and suppled on both sides of his longitudinal axis will be able to step well under himself and as close to his center of gravity as possible.

A horse that is used to going on his forehand will be much improved with a balanced transverse axis and will develop a much better

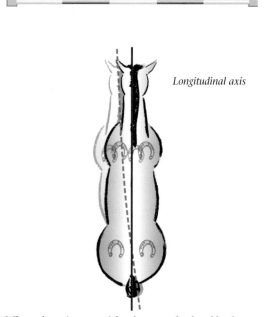

Longitudinal axis

When a horse is not straight, the power developed by the hindquarters does not go straight to the center of gravity but instead pushes the forehand to one side. If despite this, the horse tries to jump in a straight line, he has to push himself off with a unilaterally reduced force.

gitudinal and transverse axes (with the exception of when a rider shifts his weight to one side above the jump, forcing the horse to compensate). Therefore, a balanced frontal axis implies a horse is straight and accepts collection (see photo and diagram). Failing this, the rider can only bypass such a problem by always avoiding close distances.

◼ Bits and Bridles

Due to the desired responsiveness to the aids when jumping courses, riders are always looking for suitable bits and bridles. If the horse is avoiding contact or is behind the bit, it is impossible for the rider to build up positive tension when approaching a jump. On the other hand, a horse that heavily leans on the bit will often get in too close to the jump. It is a science in itself to find (or invent) a suitable bit or bridle for a specific horse. There is no limit to imagination, so for this reason, only the most popular bits and bridles are explained here.

▲ *Some horses twist their frontal axis over the jump if they reach a close takeoff distance in an unbalanced canter. In this scenario, it is helpful to improve the horse's self-carriage and carrying force with gymnastic exercises.*

foreleg technique during takeoff. In addition, they will be able to collect and compress themselves much more fluently. A horse that has learned to collect himself is better able to fly over a jump, even from a close distance.

While *above* the jump, the horse may also move his *frontal* axis: if he gets close to a rail and turns his forehand to one side, it is an indication of poor balance and instability of his lon-

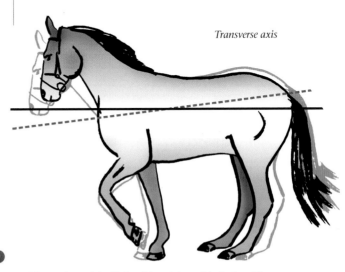

Transverse axis

A horse that originally has his weight on his forehand is better able to collect himself in front of a fence if he succeeds in balancing his transverse axis.

is that because this mouthpiece is more severe, horses avoid leaning on the bit and submit to the bit sooner, thus balancing themselves. It should be mentioned that in the United States (as compared to Germany), horses are not only ridden with more gentle hands, but the rider's influence in general is much more subtle in order to avoid making hot horses "hotter."

Single-Jointed Snaffle

This is the standard bit for schooling horses. It may be used at all levels of training. Even when problems arise, there is little risk of the rider and horse reaching an impasse. Severe mouthpieces may make a rider feel more secure, but they often only give a false impression the horse is really responsive.

Twisted Single-Jointed Full Cheek Snaffle

It is interesting that in Germany the single-jointed snaffle is the most popular mouthpiece, while in the United States, the twisted full cheek snaffle is preferred. (This bit is becoming more and more popular in Germany, as well.) The theory behind its success

A single-jointed snaffle with cheek guards to ▶ protect the corners of the horse's mouth, a flash noseband, and a running martingale. Experienced trainers return to the single-jointed snaffle when a horse has problems with contact or exhibits poor responsiveness to the aids. It guarantees sound training progress without "side effects."

Continental Gag (Pessoa) Snaffle

The pressure on the lower jaw is increased by leverage. The shorter the cheekpieces of the bridle are adjusted, the more severe is the effect of this bit. It is preferably used with horses that are either not responsive, or ones that travel with their weight on their forehand and try to balance themselves by leaning on the bit. The big disadvantage of this mouthpiece: in turns, it often has a "pinching" effect and the horse may try to evade its effect by hiding behind the bit, in which case the positive tension required for jumping cannot always be achieved.

Gag Snaffle

The gag bit is very similar to the Continental Gag in function but is tolerated more easily.

In between half-halts, the bit has to be dropped by yielding the reins in order to avoid it being drawn higher and higher into the horse's mouth.

Pelham

This bit increases pressure on the bars and under the chin. If used with a short (and therefore "sharp") curb chain, some horses are unable to show a good bascule. Because of this, it is advisable to use a loosely adjusted leather strap (similar to one that holds a spur in place), in place of the curb chain. Special care must be taken when fitting the Pelham: when the reins are pulled, the mouth of the horse should not be squeezed between the bit and curb chain. The Kimberwick bit is similar in function.

▲ *A gag snaffle with converter. Because the reins fork into two straps, the majority of the pulling force is exerted on the snaffle ring in the normal way so the mouthpiece is not drawn up as high as with a pure gag snaffle.*

▲ *This Kimberwick is very similar in function to a Pelham, but slightly more severe. The dropped noseband increases the effect.*

Hackamore

A hackamore with long "bit" cheeks can be used with horses that tense up more than desired when approaching a jump and pull too close to the fence (see photo, top right, p. 104). In this bitless bridle, many horses stop pulling against the rider's hands and into the jump; they "remain with their rider" more easily. A hackamore may also solve problems that are quite the opposite: when a horse finds even a normal mouthpiece like a snaffle so severe that he backs off from contact, a short-cheeked hackamore may help the horse gain the confidence necessary to seek contact with the rider. Other possibilities for its use include horses with teeth problems or mouth injuries, in which case a hackamore may be the only way to compete them.

▲ *This bit combines pressure on the horse's tongue and lower jaw with pressure on the nose and is similar in effect to a snaffle-hackamore combination.*

A hackamore has to be well padded (so its hinges do not pinch the horse's skin), and above all, it should not put pressure on the cheekbones when only one rein is pulled. For the same reason, the upper pieces of a good hackamore are angled away from the horse's face. It has to be adjusted in such a way that the respiratory ducts remain unaffected when the hackamore is activated; it should not exert pressure on the soft lower part of the nose. Noisy breathing or frequent blowing on the part of the horse indicates that it has been placed too low. On the other hand, if it is adjusted too high, it will pinch the cheekbones when it is activated.

In my experience, horses usually need some time to grow accustomed to this kind of bridle. So, before your form a judgment as to whether or not a hackamore is suitable for a specific horse, the horse should be given some days to become familiar with it. Some people consider a hackamore "an instrument of torture." Wrongly so, in my opinion, as the short-cheeked hackamore, in particular, is so uncomplicated and undamaging in its application that I have used it very successfully when instructing. The disadvantage is that because of the hackamore's construction, a one-sided pull on a rein is not felt by the horse in the same way it is with a snaffle. In order to compensate for this shortcoming, turns are mainly ridden with weight and leg aids—or the hackamore is combined with a snaffle bit.

Double Bridle

A double bridle consists of a curb bit, curb chain, and a bridoon (a thin snaffle). Each mouthpiece is activated by a separate pair of reins. The curb mouthpiece consists of a bar of varying thickness with a port that can be of different heights. The severity of this mouthpiece also depends upon the length of the arms of the curb and the cheekpieces and their relation to each other. To ride a horse in a double bridle, the rider has to have good control of his hands. When jumping, it is recommended that you hold the reins parallel in order to avoid the curb rein being used too strongly while in the air. When used by novice riders, the curb bit, especially, may cause the horse to hollow his back over the jump.

▩ Dropped Noseband

When compared to a flash noseband, the dropped noseband has a more severe effect. It is recommended for horses that tend to open their mouths and lean on the bit. If adjusted too low, it interferes with breathing; it should, therefore, be placed at least two fingers above the upper edge of the nostrils.

▲ *Aperio is jumped in a double bridle in order to guarantee or improve "fine tuning" in front of a jump. The severe effect of this bit is softened by short curb arms, a loose curb chain, and parallel reins.*

• • •

Regardless of the bit or bridle used, a trainer should clearly realize one thing: alternative bitting or bridling can never replace thorough, careful dressage work. Problems with contact and insufficient responsiveness to the aids are best solved by solid work on the flat in a snaffle. At the very least, this method should be the basis of one's training regimen for it minimizes the risk of training ending at a dead end. As with auxiliary reins (see below), severe bits and bridles only make sense if the trainer is actually experienced and talented enough to do without them.

▩ Auxiliary Reins

The most popular auxiliary reins for jumping are *draw reins* and *running martingales*. Much has been said and written about draw reins. They are meant to limit the possibility of the horse raising his head, but not to force flexion at the poll. However, the damage done from using them exceeds the benefit if the rider gets stuck using the reins interminably. At the jump, draw reins may serve to make the horse "jump into the rider's hand" (see "Contact," p. 49), but unless the horse is able to carry himself, this exercise is of no use whatsoever. As with severe bits, draw reins should only be used by riders who are capable of achieving their goal without them. They are, nevertheless, thought attractive and are widely used by even these perfectly capable riders because it takes less time to succeed in achieving responsiveness to the aids.

A properly adjusted *running martingale* permits the horse to raise his head, but prevents him from getting out of control. If adjusted too short, it may cause tension at

▲ *A running martingale is meant to prevent the horse from avoiding contact by lifting his head, but not all horses tolerate this auxiliary rein, especially if the straps are adjusted very short, and this may cause undesirable tension as the horse tends to "hook himself" in the martingale when approaching a jump. The full cheeks at the outside of this snaffle guarantee correct position of the bit in the horse's mouth.*

the jump, and for this reason, American riders, in particular, generally use martingales with very long straps.

Both running martingales and draw reins should not be allowed to sag between the forelegs or have big buckles because a horse might catch a leg or a hoof when tucking up his forelegs over the fence.

Of course there is a much wider range of auxiliary reins offered by the equestrian industry. However, I would rather not offer a more detailed explanation as, in my opinion, they are irrelevant for the honest training of a quality jumper. Good riding cannot be replaced by anything else!

▪ Expression of Harmony

One of the unspoken higher goals of equitation, maybe even the ethical justification for riding at all (see "Training and Ethics," p. 147) is the expression of congenial mutual attachment between man and mount, a feeling of being bound to one another. Responsiveness to the aids is the means to reach this goal when jumping a course, but there is one fundamental idea that must not be missed for all that dressage work is worth (see sidebar on p. 77).

▲ *Show jumping is not only about "jumping a number of colored obstacles without faults as quickly as possible." One of the unspoken goals is the expression of attachment between horse and rider.*

The essence of jumping is in riding *forward*, not *backward*. Jumping lives on dynamics—on the flow of motion.

I have an interesting little story in this context: "Sepp" Gemein, an excellent rider and at one point coach of young riders throughout his region of Germany, was training an ambitious young man who had started his riding career in dressage and now wanted to do show jumping. Many would think he had an ideal background, but it actually proved to be the opposite. The way he rode did not allow for the dynamics or lightness of forward movement. Sepp dryly summed it up in one sentence, "How I would love to take this fellow to the racetrack for a morning workout!" Indeed, the image of a jockey perfectly adapting himself to the motion of a galloping horse, absorbing his power, and guiding him without interference—this is the true nature of jumping.

Compared to other equestrian disciplines, horses for jumping may represent the widest variety of types and breeds. They may be light or heavy, smart or awkward, sensitive or sturdy or unruly, but all of them may develop into top jumpers if there is some genius in their actual talent for jumping fences. This is to say that a jumper rider must deal with a much wider variety of types and characters than, say, a dressage rider. But, as he does not have to ride a "test" (he just needs the fastest round without faults) and may avail himself of a wider variety of bits and auxiliary reins, he has more possibilities of being capable of adapting himself to an individual horse.

As far as rideability is concerned, there is hardly anything I would not forgive a horse.

HELENA WEINBERG
The Hannoveraner, August, 2002

Jump Training

As I've mentioned, the dressage work described in the previous chapter is not an end in itself. Its purpose is to enable the horse to develop his jumping abilities. The goal will always be to jump a round without faults. This is where horse and rider are in their element.

Jumping Technique

There are more contradictory views on the ideal way of jumping than one can imagine.

Aperio's sire A Priori (ridden by the author) jumped with a lot of bascule and buoyancy, tucking his forearms up relatively high. ▼

The demands on a horse's jumping style depend on his use. A hunter jumps differently than a Grand Prix jumper or an amateur's horse. The ideal jumping process, as it is favored in green horse divisions, may be described as follows: from a generous, rhythmical, uphill canter, a supple and relaxed jump should develop, one that demonstrates confidence, control, and intelligence. This means that after resolutely collecting himself for a moment, the horse should—without any hesitation—energetically push off the ground, quickly tucking up his forelegs (the forearms should be lifted near the horizontal, and the cannon bone should remain close to the forearm until after the last rail). A powerful takeoff and generous space between the horse's body and the highest rail are desirable; however, his jumping should be sensible and energy efficient.

Ideally, the horse lifts his back over the fence, his withers protruding and neck sloping slightly downward (his *bascule*). The ideal climax of the jump trajectory depends on the kind of fence: over a vertical, it will lie exactly over the highest rail; over a parallel, it is over the "middle" between the front and the back element; over a triple bar, it is over the last rail. Strongly angled hind joints are not considered as favorable as a slight "kicking up" or "opening up" of the hindquarters, which demonstrates scope (although it must not affect the horse's balance). The landing should be fluent and light-footed, on a straight line, and should merge into the former rhythm of the canter without loss of impulsion.

Uses

As is the case of conformation, there are many elite jumpers that do not fit into this "ideal" jumping picture. Though it may be true that most riders would be delighted to have a horse that jumps in the described manner, the most important condition is the horse's disposition, or mental attitude. Cautiousness, focus, and a competitive nature have to be given priority over technique and bascule. In fact, if a horse appears too "rounded" over smallish fences, it is a typical indication of limited scope. And, if he tucks his head back and "peeks" down at the fence (as is seen time and again in sales photographs) this bascule is actually the result of fear and tension.

Nevertheless, if the jumping process can be improved, it may make all the difference

Jumping style does not dictate the quality of the horse. It's Otto, ridden here by Geoff Billington, was one of the best jumpers of his time although his bascule and foreleg technique—as seen here—were far from ideal. ▼

between a talented and a really brilliant jumper. Logically, the manner in which the horse should jump depends on the kind of competition he is mainly used for. As you know, there are not only Grand Prix competitions (even though every breeder of performance horses is thinking of his "Olympic horse" when planning his matches). For example, a puissance horse needs scope and courage more than anything else. He does not need ideal jumping technique and certainly needn't be at all cautious. For a speed horse, it is important to be quick with the forelegs, but also to be supple, clever, and controlled. He does not need nearly the scope a puissance horse should possess, and if mounted by an excellent rider, he does not even need as much courage.

A good horse for an amateur rider should possess more talents: he should be naturally balanced (actively stepping close to his center of gravity) and "pull" his rider toward the jump. Horses with an active canter stride and a naturally keen personality are favored because amateur riders are not yet able to really influence the horse's balance or propelling forces. In addition, a classic amateur's horse should be able, time and again, to compensate for any of his rider's faults and to see the desirable takeoff point by himself. To this purpose, the horse's ability of organizing his last few strides before the jump is more important than the actual takeoff point. This ability of "seeing his stride" is mainly inherited and can be trained only to a small degree. The better the rider, the more he will take over and influence the last strides, but in a really difficult situation, even a top rider is glad to have a horse that is able to assist.

The ability to quickly tuck up the

forelegs and jump even from half a stride without faults and without losing impulsion is also necessary. Moreover, the horse should not be too "rounded" over the jump. Inexperienced riders are not very fond of horses with too much bascule because they tend to feel insecure over the jump.

Bascule

A good natural bascule may be negatively affected by lack of suppleness, poor responsiveness to the aids, or improper rider influence. If, for example, the rider tries to "lift" his horse over the jump by pulling on the reins, the horse will hollow his back more and more, and his front cannon bones will hang down vertically over the jump instead of being tucked up close to the forearms. It would be better to avoid the faults made by the front legs by balancing the horse, as this does not impair the bascule. George Morris describes this as follows:

> *If the rider shifts his own center of gravity further back…the horse will simultaneously lift his head and neck and thus shift his center of gravity further back as well. This is exactly what we want. The lighter the horse is in his forehand and the more angled his haunches are, the freer and more agile his forelegs become.*[23]

I do not completely agree with this concept. The goal may be the same, but according to the classical rules, relative elevation is achieved by increasing the carrying power of the hindquarters. We should try to increase the elevation of head and neck by lowering the haunches to a certain degree, not vice versa. Of course, I must acknowledge that the American jumping style implies a much more forward canter when approaching a fence than is the custom in Europe. The horses that correspond to this particular style will often collect themselves of their own accord within the last few strides.

If a horse approaches a fence in a collected and balanced manner and is carrying himself, the takeoff point can be closer to the fence without worry about a knock down. The horse can remain supple in his back. Most horses need to strengthen their carrying forces to enable them to take off from a short distance—few are naturally able to preserve impulsion when taking off close to a fence at the beginning of schooling.

In order to improve the bascule, you can sometimes lay a plank painted in striking colors just beyond the fence—preferably a wall or another "densely filled" obstacle—and before the probable landing point. In mid-trajectory, the horse suddenly sees the plank and in a reflex movement will bascule. But, this does not produce a long-term effect. Another means of improving the bascule is a grid consisting of a row of parallels. However, while it is true that the bascule is easily spoiled by poor rider aids, it is rarely improved to any extent that exceeds the horse's natural talent.

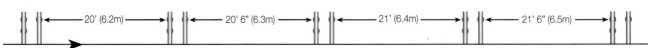

For horses that have a tendency to not bascule under saddle, a good exercise is to approach a row of parallels from a slightly collected canter. This has additional positive effects on rhythm, foreleg technique, and focus.

---

[23] Morris, George, *The American Jumping Style*, New York: Doubleday, 1993.

Foreleg Technique

Fortunately, unlike the bascule, foreleg technique is easier to improve. As mentioned before, the decisive factor is whether carrying power and bascule have already been developed. If so, they may be put into use at the jump.

■ Dangling Cannon Bones

Many young horses jump their first few fences with their front cannon bones hanging more or less vertically down over the jump. In an early stage of training, this does not mean that they are not careful enough or are lacking in technique. Most horses only learn to fold their legs close to the forearms when fences become higher or after having knocked down some rails. If an experienced horse drops his cannon bones at the top of his trajectory and "feels" for the height of

▲ *Crossing the fore or hind legs (see p. 85) is seldom seen and is a bad habit, but does not usually cause more knock-downs or falls. Stretched-out forelegs as well (as seen here) may only be due to the horse's individual jumping style, and do not necessarily indicate an emergency scramble to salvage a jump.*

the rails, there are four possible reasons:

1. He is not careful enough by nature.
2. His routine has made him careless.
3. The rider consistently chooses a long takeoff point.
4. It is his personal jumping style and cannot be altered.

There are very careful horses that jump with dangling cannon bones all their lives.

◄ *An "open" foreleg—the cannon bones hanging more or less vertically down, perpendicular to the forearms—is characteristic of inexperienced or careless jumpers. It may also be caused by the rider if he always asks the horse to take off from a rather long distance (as is the case in hunter classes where such a foreleg technique is desired).*

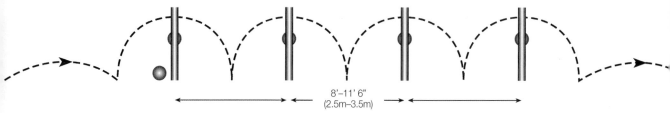

8'–11' 6"
(2.5m–3.5m)

An in-and-out row encourages "quicker legs" and improves coordination between the forehand and hindquarters. Very short distances force the horse to push off the ground in split seconds without elongating his body. This exercise requires extreme effort and can only be required of horses capable of collecting themselves.

This may be not be the most economical way of jumping as they have to jump higher in order not to touch the rails, but if they are reliable jumpers, any rider will tolerate it. A similar habit is jumping with crossed forelegs—it looks spectacular, but there is no risk involved.

▪ Stretched-Out Forelegs

This foreleg technique has the following causes:

1. If a horse is made to approach a spread without impulsion or take off from too far away, he may stretch his forelegs in an attempt to clear the obstacle.

2. If the demands being made are close to the horse's limit, some will stretch their forelegs, even if the takeoff point is correct.

3. In rare cases, "scopey" horses stretch their forelegs unnecessarily, thus underlining their individual character. Famous examples of this style are Snowbound (Bill Steinkraus), Myntha (Helena Lundbeck), and Milton (John Whitaker).

▪ "Leaving a Leg"

Sometimes young horses lift one forearm in the takeoff and leave the other dangling.

This happens almost exclusively when a takeoff point is very close to the fence or when the horse is restrained by the rider in his approach. In equestrian slang, we speak of "leaving a leg." A horse that shows a tendency to do this should be trained to deal with short takeoffs with the help of properly placed ground poles or by pulling out the lower elements of the fence.

In-and-out rows also help with this problem. They encourage "quicker legs" and improve coordination between the forehand and hindquarters. Such a row is approached from a collected canter, and the more collection a horse is able to master, the closer the distances can be chosen. If the rider keeps his horse on the bit while jumping the in-and-outs and does not transfer too much of his weight to his thighs and knees (maintains the light seat), the distances within the row may be as short as 8 feet (2.5m). Height and length of the row depends on the stage of training and the abilities of both horse and rider.

Safety cups should be used with these in-and-outs in order to prevent the horse from catching his hind leg on the top rail (see "Fences and Course Design," p. 124). If safety cups are not at hand, position the rails on the edges of the cups in order to avoid a bad accident. This exercise is extremely strenuous.

Some faults made by the forelegs seem

incomprehensible to the rider who may say, "Until then, he jumped so well, and then all of a sudden, he stretched out one front leg!" Of course, such things happen sometimes. Or, perhaps at the previous jump the horse folded up his forelegs to such an extreme that he knocked them against his chest, and in order to avoid pain at the next jump, he stretched out one leg and knocked down a rail. (A well padded chest protector can help avoid this type of fault. It should fit close to the body as light rails in flat cups can be easily dislodged by one that is hanging loosely.) Or, maybe the horse forged a front shoe with a hind leg during takeoff, in which case he should be shod appropriately and fitted with overreach boots.

Explosive Takeoff

Horses that are a bit slow in takeoff can be trained over a ground pole placed before the last stride in front of the fence. If the rider increases his forward driving aids

A ground pole for the last stride before takeoff encourages the horse to push off the ground in an energetic and explosive manner.

8'–10" (2.5m–3m)   10' (3m)

at the takeoff, a more explosive takeoff can be achieved. Hugo Simon, for one, was a fervent advocate of this technique. In order to avoid too close a takeoff point, leg pressure should not be applied until the forelegs have touched the ground in their last stride. In this way, only the hindquarters are encouraged further forward so the trajectory becomes *higher* instead of *longer*. The rider should not shift his upper body too far forward nor yield the reins too early. A giving hand is required only at the top of the trajectory in order not to disturb the bascule.

This kind of assistance should only be given to horses familiar with the collecting aids and ones that do not generally tend to jump explosively forward.

Despite all the possible ways of influencing the jumping process, we should always try to avoid extremes. The warning expressed by a senior instructor of the Spanish Riding School of Vienna in the middle of the nineteenth century applies to today's jumping competitions as well:

Abuse by exaggerated and consistent use of force is of no benefit; it has a paralyzing effect and ruins all efforts; in other words, this use of force only results in apathy and total dullness toward the aids.

GRAF MONTIGNY

"Paddling"

A very serious and unpleasant mistake is "paddling" over a spread. When the horse is afraid of not being able to jump wide enough to clear the jump, he tries to find the ground by stretching out one foreleg—or both—over the jump. Usually, the last rail is then knocked down, but worse, it may cause a nasty fall as the last rail is generally caught between the forelegs, preventing a safe landing. This faulty technique is genetic. Horses like Ratina (Beerbaum/Raymakers) or For Pleasure (Nieberg/Ehning) would

▲ *The fatal tendency of trying to solve problems by "paddling" is generally inherited. For Pleasure has great scope and knows it—and therefore he would never "paddle," however far the last rail of a spread or parallel might be.*

probably never paddle, however wide the spread might seem, but L'Eperon (Kreutz-mann/Nagel) and Cassini (Sloothaak), had to struggle with this problem time and again.

The rider of such a mount can only try to accustom his horse to a trajectory that is wide rather than steep during warm-up. Moreover, he should always try to keep the horse "in front of him," and he should not participate in competitions that push the limit. There is no direct connection between limited scope and paddling. Rather, it may actually be a sign of the horse's competitive spirit.

Hind Leg Technique

The natural technique of the hind legs can be influenced by the aids only to a small degree. Rather, the goal should be to maintain the same technique under saddle that the horse displays while free jumping.

Horses with a tendency to "paddle" are potentially ▶ *dangerous. L'Eperon (ridden by Carsten-Otto Nagel) displays this habit at the last element of a long-distance combination at the Hickstead European Championships.*

▲ *Normally angled hind legs* ▲

▲ *Hind legs that "open up" over the jump are not absolutely necessary but do indicate an elastic body.*

▲ *Crossing the hind legs is not a major disadvantage, although precautions against potential injury should be taken by fitting the horse with boots or bandages.*

▲ *Horses with a strong fighting spirit may occasionally kick out over the jump. This habit usually doesn't present much of a problem (it is almost impossible to correct) and is only annoying if the horse happens to kick down a rail at the same time.*

Shifting the Hind Legs Sideways

When a rider consistently shifts his weight to one side, he forces his mount to compensate for this. As a result, the horse often shifts his hind legs to the same side.

Applying Driving Aids

When jumping obstacles of a certain height, the rider should be able to apply driving aids in the takeoff. If he consistently jumps paral-

It was an interesting experience when at the end of the eighties John Whitaker paused at Paul Schockemöhle's barn in Mühlen, Germany, between two horse shows. Everybody on the grounds, employees and all, were keen to sneak some hints or information from such a world-class rider. The best horses were saddled for him, Deister, among others. Deister had a technique of tilting his hindquarters to one side over jumps. John jumped him and then said he would not have been able to improve the horse in any way. The characteristic "tilt" was, in his opinion, connected with Paul's habit of always leaning to one side over the jump. At the 1982 World Championships in Dublin, this jumping style had consequences for Deister's rider: at a bow-shaped obstacle, Deister knocked down own of the higher side elements when he tilted his hindquarters as usual. It was this fault that excluded them from the final four for the World Championship.

lels or triple bars without them, the jumping process will deteriorate as a rule: the horse stretches out his forelegs earlier or "feels"

Champion du Lys is the opposite of a power jumper, but compensates for lack of power with technique: before taking off, he "makes himself smaller"—he "dives" in front of the fence, lowers his haunches, and thus develops more jumping power. ▼

for the last rail; impulsion is lost, and the jump is not "finished"; and the jumping process no longer conveys the impression of scope. It may even result in the hind legs being drawn under the belly, or being "dropped into" the spread for a split second.

If, in spite of correctly applied aids, the hind legs are drawn under the belly, the horse is not "scopey" enough to deal with the tasks at hand. Similar to paddling, this phenomenon is seen in combinations with long distances (where takeoff point and speed cannot always be optimized), and occasionally, the hind legs are dropped into the parallel or spread. Although this happens for the same reasons as paddling with the forelegs, there is no risk of a fall, and it is, therefore, a minor fault.

Faults of the hind legs are more often encountered in speed competitions. After a long stretch of cantering, the horse is not elevated enough, and as a result, the trajectory becomes wide and flat. Attention is exclusively focused on tucking up the forelegs as quickly as possible, while the hind legs are not tucked up quickly enough. Even when jumping against the clock, the rider should remain sufficiently in control in order to rebalance his horse before a fence after a stretch of fast canter. In addition, he should be aware that the higher the speed, the wider the horse's trajectory becomes, so after a prolonged stretch of cantering, sufficient room should be left for the takeoff. And, the rider should avoid shifting his weight too far forward, as this also makes for a flat trajectory.

■ Tricks for "Opening-Up"

In recent years, it has become somewhat fashionable to improve "opening-up" (not folding the hind legs up too soon over the jump) by other means, such as weighting brushing boots with lead reinforcement, or overtightening the boots on the hind legs. With some horses the effect of this is actually surprising: they focus on their hind legs and indeed open up more, and the jumping process appears much more spectacular. But be careful: sensitive horses may be easily irritated and refuse. In addition, both the division of power from front and hind legs throughout the course, and the balance over the jump are impeded (sometimes resulting in the forelegs compensating and being stretched out too early).

This one example of a jumper rider's tricks may suffice. It is the intention of this book to deal with the training of the jumping horse, not strive for short-term effect. But, although solid basic training is the topic, one thing should be absolutely clear: in the long run, the basic quality of a horse cannot be improved by the training abilities of a rider, as varied and imaginative as they may be. They can only be used to develop natural talents of a horse that are already in place.

Total Process

As said earlier, before the total process of jumping can be improved, the dressage requirements have to be fulfilled. It is of no use to try to influence the jumping technique if the horse is not supple and controllable in any situation before or after the jump. You cannot expect a horse to take off energetically if his movements lack impulsion or if balance or straightness are missing.

■ Taking Off Too Early

The desirable takeoff point should be determined as inconspicuously as possible. A skillful rider guides his mount toward the fence in such a way that the horse recognizes the takeoff point chosen by the rider as the only one possible. For this to happen, the rider needs a good eye and a relatively responsive horse. Lack of responsiveness to the aids is often the reason why young horses take off too early, which occurs when horses, having become tense, rush their fences, and take a stronger contact in front of the jump. It is this tension that causes young horses to choose an early takeoff point—to jump "big." When this happens, training should be focussed on suppleness and balance in front of the jump. Jumping from the trot, ground poles in front of the fence, and distances that are not too tight help make the horse understand the desired number of canter strides.

■ Taking Off Too Close

It is different with horses that take off too close to the fence. This is always a sign of uncertainty and frequently happens with horses mounted by novice riders. These horses do not dare jump early because they anticipate painful jabs in their mouths or other discomfort, sometimes delaying takeoff even when the correct point is reached. Even if they are eventually ridden by a rider who sees his stride, it may take months until they dare jump confidently on a regular basis.

For the purpose of correcting this habit, the fence's ground line can be pulled a bit away from the fence to make it easier for the horse to recognize the correct takeoff point (preferably a medium to fairly short distance). In the approach, the horse should remain in front of the leg—there should be distinct contact up to, and during, the take-

off. This helps avoid a situation that allows the horse to insert an extra canter stride. The horse's trust in his rider will gradually increase until an earlier takeoff point (always with the ground line pulled out) can be chosen. Impulsion is essential and should not be lost under any circumstance.

Horses that are naturally careless may sometimes become inattentive if the rider always gets the takeoff point right. They feel all too safe possibly thinking, "The guy up there will find me a comfortable takeoff; I don't have to do it myself!" Those horses will get more interested in their job if they are occasionally required to "see" their stride for themselves, and their concentration can be even more improved if "seeing" the takeoff point is made challenging (see "Alertness Education," p. 90).

■ "Body Jumping"

If a young horse arches his body too high above the jump, this is generally a sign of carefulness and is therefore favored by experienced riders. They know that with a growing training routine and habituation, the jumping process will become more economical. The basic prerequisite is suppleness and trust in the rider.

There is, however, a certain type of horse that prefers to jump too high all his life, though with dangling forelegs. Recently, the most popular example of this type was Tomboy, ridden by Rodrigo Pessoa. As long as this jumping technique is performed with careful precision, it is not necessarily a disadvantage (even though Pessoa missed out winning the World Cup Finals in 1997 because of Tomboy's enormous jumps). Of course, a jumping technique that involves jumping a couple of feet higher at each fence is less economical and increases wear and tear, so such horses do not only need more power, but also more endurance than others.

■ Belly Gliding

If there is too little space between the horse's body and the top rail, wide parallels should be jumped from a collected gait. Jumping from the walk may also help to adjust the trajectory "upward." The horse should be ridden in a loose and relaxed walk toward the fence, and only during the last few strides should positive body tension be built up. The horse is "driven into the rider's hand" until the hind legs have left the ground. If the reins are yielded too early, the horse may feel insecure and may hesitate. This kind of approach and takeoff encourages a steeper trajectory. Moreover, it makes "electric" horses (those with natural impulsion that has not yet been cultivated) more controllable and teaches them to focus.

Sometimes the problem of a horse using his body too little when jumping is homemade: the rider allows the horse to accelerate of his own accord after the jump, and consequently, the following jumps become flatter. It is fine for a young horse to move at will after the jump and thus release tension. (It is also normal for such horses to become disunited after jumping.) But, this tendency should not be encouraged by letting the horse run off in an uncontrolled way. The more training progresses, the more important it becomes to rebalance the horse after each jump.

■ Dynamic Jumping Process

If impulsion is lost at takeoff, it may help to accelerate repeatedly directly after the jump. Also, in extreme cases, the whip or crop can be applied either during the takeoff or when above the fence. In this case, the takeoff point should not be too close. The rider should also pay attention to keeping the horse collected, not letting him become "too long" when approaching the jump. The rider should keep up contact—frame in the horse with his aids—or the horse may become hesitant, lack confidence, and not develop the desired vigor at the jump.

■ "Heavy Landing"

When a horse loses impulsion upon landing, we speak of a "heavy landing." Although predisposed to a certain genetic disposition (heavy Warmbloods, for example) this can also be a sign of lack of fitness or overexertion. In the case of extremely careful horses, the reason may be that they spend too much energy on the jump itself. The trainer should then take care to make jumping as comfortable as possible. For example:

● Ride with consistent speed and to a takeoff point that is not too close
● Be efficient (as a rule, heavy aids result in the horse expending extra effort)
● Build training jumps with easy spreads and heights
● Begin with easy, acclimatizing courses when planning a competition schedule
● Plan to move from frequent easy tasks to occasional more demanding courses throughout the season

If the horse is neither overworked nor tense, a cavaletti placed at its highest measure or a single ground pole placed 9' 6" to 11' 6" (3m to 3.5m) after a small parallel may encourage a smoother landing.

Finishing the Jump

If the horse's bascule does not last long enough or he stretches out his forelegs too early so that he "gropes" for the back rail when landing, we say the horse is "not finishing his jump." To correct this fault, the horse should be trained to jump spreads with a lower front rail from the collected canter and a short takeoff point. Thus, the horse is encouraged to focus on the back rail. When this has been repeated frequently and successfully, the session may be concluded by finally tackling parallel bars. The front rail may be knocked down at the first attempt, but the horse's attention soon will be focused on both front and back rails at the same time, thus improving his bascule and the way he opens up over the jump.

The complete jumping process is often improved by a lively "forward moving" course as can be seen in the United States where fluid rounds are promoted by the course design itself. Jumping grounds are usually spacious, the fences are placed far from each other, and in competition, parallels hardly ever consist of truly parallel bars. In the approach to the fence, the horse is unrestrained—he is not "held together" as in Europe, but instead may carry his head and neck as he thinks comfortable. To be successful, this horse has to be wide-awake, but often times is actually smarter, jumps with much scope, and is relaxed and supple in manner.

Alertness Education

Faults such as a listless, powerless takeoff may creep in if training is overdone or becomes too monotonous. "There must always be something happening underneath me," Franke Sloothaak once aptly remarked.

A horse will only learn successfully if he is in a fresh and enterprising mood; exhaustion and monotony will only result in carelessness. Work should always be varied to awaken the interest and attention of the horse.[24]

According to Franke Sloothaak, "the horse should always respect the fence a bit more than the rider." This is why during training a rider should not always avoid a knock-down by fully supporting his horse over the fence. The occasional knock-down encourages a horse to focus for himself to avoid a fault. Jumping should be easy for the horse; he should not tighten up from sheer effort. With an experienced horse that has become negligent, it may be useful occasionally to remove the ground line during training or in the warm-up to gain his attention. In addition, leave his boots open in the front. The horse should be aware of touching a rail so he can learn from his mistake. Experience and sensitivity are always necessary to train well and with success.

Training Natural Fences

Xenophon's principle, "Teach the easy before the difficult" is of particular importance when training a horse to jump rustic looking obstacles. Time and again riders, deceived by the ease with which their horses jump verticals and parallels, are utterly surprised to find their horses hesitate—or even refuse—when approaching natural fences of the same degree of difficulty. Maybe these riders found it too much of a hassle to drive to another facility where they could train over natural fences; whatever the reason, the result is a

---

[24] Smith, Harvey, *Show Jumping*, London: TTT Ltd., 1979 (p. 49).

situation that is too much for the horse to handle, and his basic trust in his rider is shaken.

Unfortunately, natural fences are rarely included in today's course designs as they no longer correspond to increased safety demands. Or, they are avoided by riders because they are so difficult and result in many refusals. If small water ditches, banks or trakehners (dry ditches) were more often found in young horse divisions, possibly fewer problems would arise later on.

For the advanced training of jumpers, the schooling of trakehners and banks belong to the "work of diligence" category. At first, small and easy examples should be jumped before more tricky designs are tackled. The rider should take care to maintain positive body tension until the horse's hindquarters have left the ground. If the reins are yielded too early, an inexperienced or timid jumper may suddenly feel left alone and hesitate.

Water Ditches

A water ditch is a common test for five-year-olds starting out in competition. Usually, there are two basic problems: the horse either respects the water too much, or too little. With young jumpers, we are mainly confronted with representatives of the first group so the task is to help the horse overcome his fear. For this type, riding by and through small streams and puddles may initially help overcome a good deal of timidity.

A transportable rubber ditch is very practical, especially when such an obstacle is introduced for the first time. It does not appear as awe-inspiring as a solid natural obstacle and is not as risky should the horse happen to step inside. During training, a water ditch should be jumped with raised rails above it. A timid horse feels safer because the obstacle looks more familiar than a flat ditch. And, by using rails, those jumpers that have too little respect for

◄ *The marked ground line and the "wings" provide optical orientation for this young horse. If a ditch is jumped as respectfully as is shown here, there is no need for a raised rail across. However, if the horse does not take off energetically and prolongs his stride, a rail across the hind third of the ditch may help.*

water (and don't mind getting their feet wet) learn to land after the back edge of the ditch. With these types of horses, water ditches should not be schooled too often in order to keep their attention fresh for competition. Streams and puddles should always be bypassed when hacking out to preserve a certain respect for water.

Basic speed is increased in the approach to water, and the takeoff point should be close to the front edge of the ditch. In spite of the increased speed necessary for a wide jump, it is essential for the rider to be "pulled" with the horse's positive body tension toward the jump (thus keeping the horse "in front of him"). If he neglects this principle, a timid or very careful horse may feel left alone and refuse. This stage of training should be taken very seriously from the beginning. Once a sensitive horse has lost

confidence, he may have a "water problem" for the rest of his life.

> **Giulietta was a horse that overcame a "water problem" thanks to skillful riding. Her previous owner, a very successful and strong young rider, had traded her to Paul Schockemöhle because (among other reasons) the mare had a deep-rooted aversion to water ditches. In order to give her the necessary confidence, it was essential for her rider not to "override" her and to keep her in front of his leg. She would then trust her rider—but still respected the water enough to always land far beyond the white line. Later on, she became so safe that my brother rode her successfully in several Nations Cups.**

A ditch without a visual reference can be overwhelming, and an easy clearance of such an obstacle can only be expected from a very experienced horse. ▼

When tackling frightening obstacles with a young horse for the first time, use the herd instinct: an experienced horse takes the lead and "pulls" the inexperienced one over the jump. The distance between the two horses should not be more than shown here. ▼

▲ *The back edge of ditches should be fitted with a non-slip, shock-absorbing material. In this case, a perforated rubber mat was used.*

attempt, the horse should be given the impression that the task is easy to solve. Later on, if big ditches of, say, 13 feet (4m) wide have to be schooled, place a small hedge in front of the water to increase the distance.

The construction of the back edge of the ditch should not be angled too steeply down and it should be made of non-slip, shock-absorbing material. Moreover, the water should reach the edge so the edge of the jump is clearly visible and the horse learns not to step on the white line that marks it.

If water problems are schooled too often and too aggressively, it may result in the horse looking for a ditch under every fence. It is better to make use of the herd instinct (i.e. have an experienced horse take the lead), avoid force, and occasionally insert the task into the daily routine. In this way, jumping water is no longer associated with stress and tension.

It is essential to consider where and how to build a solid water ditch. Young horses will find it easier to jump the ditch in the direction of the arena exit, toward the stable. Hedges or wings positioned on either side of the water give optical support. Moreover, the ditch should have a good width (the distance from left to right) so that the horse sees no opportunity of running out, and it should not be too deep (from front to back). From his first

▲ *The ears of the horse reveal some doubt on his part: is there a ditch underneath the next fence, or is it simply that the distance in the combination is just a little long? In any case, determination on the rider's part and courage on the horse's are required.*

Combinations and "Distances"

Before combinations and "distances" are schooled, the horse must be able to remain in balance and on the bit after landing. Otherwise, the rider will be unable to influence the horse between the jumps. To prepare, jump a single vertical followed by a turn, and then jump the same vertical again from the other side. When this is done several times, it will be clear if the horse becomes more willing to accept restraining aids after the jump. Next, build a sequence of fences (see diagram below) to offer some variation.

should not disturb the natural flow of movement. In the case of tight combinations or distances, care should be taken to ensure that the last stride can be finished before the jumps. The required shortening of the last stride should correspond to the degree of collection already reached in flatwork, otherwise tension, loss of impulsion, and hesitation are the result.

When schooling "long" distances, be sure the horse is not frightened or tensed up, which could cause him to flatten his trajectory. With inexperienced horses, pay attention to the canter lead between fences.

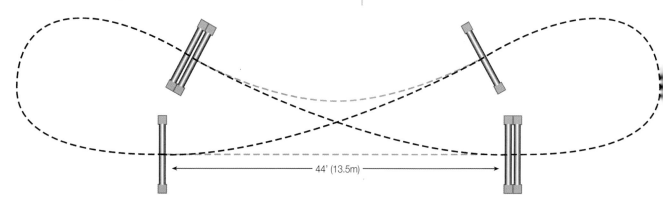

This design requires little material and construction effort and provides various possibilities of schooling different fences in both directions.

44' (13.5m)

By alternating between straight lines and turns, the young horse learns to keep his rhythm, even in a relatively small indoor arena. The more training progresses, the more varied the sequences of fences and their distances may become (they no longer have to be placed at the optimum distances, see p. 95). After all, it does not make sense to always jump ideal distances when the horse will be confronted with varying distances in competition. But, they should always be equal to the stage of training and the horse's ability, and they

Directly after landing, the horse has to be collected again with leg and rein aids in order to avoid him becoming insecure.

Some horses have problems with a relatively high vertical as the first element in a combination. Their front leg technique becomes uncertain, they twist their bodies or they do not get enough height. This problem cannot always be solved by training, as the ability to cope with a vertical first element is an inborn talent.

A ditch with a raised rail above should also, from time to time, be included in a small combination during training to avoid difficulty in competition later on. Overcareful or spooky horses may sometimes find this stage of training problematic (see "Resistance," p. 108). Triple combinations should be part of the routine, as well. For a talented horse that has already mastered a double combination, this does not create a real problem. Gridwork has made him familiar with a row of several fences, so a triple—or even quadruple—combination with suitable distances should not be difficult for the horse. However, it can be for the rider: he has to figure out how to tackle the combination and be able to give the right aids at the right moment (speed, takeoff point, and trajectory).

When the distances between the elements of a triple combination are awkward, responsive horses and secure riders are required, though usually, only participants in more advanced jumping classes are faced with this kind of problem. Generally speaking, course demands should correspond to the horse's present stage of training and not cause strain. There are too many examples of top horses whose careers did not reach their potential because they were forced to jump difficult course designs too early.

Jumping difficult double and triple combinations is, of course, also a question of experience. In the beginning of their careers, Banhui del Follee and Power Light used to "feel" for the top rail of the first element with their forelegs. They were insecure and tried to do the second "step" before the first one, stretching out their forelegs although they had not yet "finished" the jump. Both got over this bad habit with practice. They even became real combination specialists: they recognized and solved situations whether the distances within the jumps were long or short.

As a result of the improved conditions in jumping competition (better breeding, better riding, better footing, lighter course construction), the ideal distances have been enlarged to some degree. According to course designer Olaf Petersen, the average canter stride can nowadays be calculated to be 12 feet (3.7m). Starting from a two-stride distance of 35' 6" (10.8m), the rider only has to add in his mind 12 feet (3.7m) for any additional stride in order to be able to calculate the number of strides required for a spe-

5' (150cm)　24' 6" (7.5m)　3' (90cm)　4' 6" (145cm)　29' (8.8m)　4' 6" (145cm)　5' (150cm)

Olympic Games, Rome, 1960—triple combination

4' 6" (145cm)　5' (150cm)　26' (7.9m)　5' (155cm)　33' (10.1m)　2' (70cm)　5' (155cm)

"Substitute" Olympic Games, Rotterdam, 1980—triple combination

Bad examples from jumping history: there is hardly a horse that can solve such extreme distances; they are unfair and destroy the basis of jumping—the horse's trust. (Feet measurements above are approximate.)

cific distance (47' 6" for three strides; 59' 6" for four strides; and so on). In addition, it has to be taken into account that smaller fences do require a shorter trajectory than bigger ones. But, it is not only the tape that measures whether a distance is right or not.

The following factors contribute to making a distance or sequence of fences *longer*:

- Deep footing
- Line leading uphill
- Line leading away from an exit
- Impressive solid construction (such as a wall)
- Horse that has a small "engine"
- Beginning of the round (horse has not yet "got going")
- Parallel jump/ parallel combination (difficult trajectory)
- Triple bar as the last element (shorter takeoff point)
- Frightening "spooky" fence as the last element
- Small show ground or arena
- First element jumped out of a sharp turn
- Fence close to the arena wall
- Tight sequence of fences immediately prior

And these characteristics make distances *shorter*:

- Line leading downhill
- Sequence of fences leading toward the exit
- Horse has a big "engine"

- Final phase of a jump-off or speed competition
- Large show ground or arena
- Longer distance fence sequence immediately prior
- Triple bar or water ditch as first element of a sequence
- Two-stride combinations
- Sequence of fences *with* change of rein (from the right in a bend to the left, for example)

To which degree the course conditions (instead of the tape measure) decide whether a distance is right or not is seen at the CHIO Aachen, Germany, year after year. At the Aachen show ground, elements in a combination can be placed over 3 feet (1m) further apart without appearing really long. The spacious arena and good footing encourage the horses to canter much more freely than at other grounds.

Power Light at the Aachen Grand Prix, ridden by Alois Pollmann-Schweckhorst ▶

Jumping a Course

Even if every difficult individual aspect of a course has been mastered during training, no such exercise can replace the true reality check: jumping a real course. It would be ideal to be able to transfer the horse to an unknown jumping ground with good footing and good fence material in order to be able to imitate competitive conditions. If need be, jumping a course can also be trained at home, but the rider should spend some time and effort to transport the horse to encounter a change of fence constructions. Having to cope with continually changing fences and course lines makes the horse fit for the demands of competition.

If possible, the course should first be inspected on foot. Walking the course is an essential part of the mental preparation for competition. A meticulous mental analysis of all the steps necessary results in continuity.[25] This regularity is, in turn, the prerequisite for conditioning a horse.

The Warm-Up

Preparation in the warm-up area can be organized as follows: first, the dressage criteria according to the Training Scale are checked and refreshed; then, a small vertical or crossrail is approached. Special attention is focused on suppleness; only those muscles absolutely necessary for the jump should be tightened, and then immediately relaxed again. This phase should not be underestimated, as every top performance is based on suppleness.

When peak responsiveness to the aids is established (the horse remains on the bit and in balance before, as well as after the jump), the vertical may be raised. The rider should now try to transform the horse's semicircle trajectory into a semi-oval one. If he succeeds, he can approach a small parallel with the back rail slightly higher than the front rail. The horse's attention should be focused on the back rail until he develops the forward impulse necessary for a spread. This teaches the horse to keep his front legs tucked up long enough and to "open up" (see "Total Process," p. 87). Next, jump a true parallel (with actual parallel rails) and the horse's focus should be guided to the front rail, as well. If the parallel is successfully jumped, take a break and allow the horse to relax. Before entering the ring, jump a higher fence once in order to make sure the horse is attentive and ready for the tasks at hand.

This preparation may vary, according to the type of horse. It should be directed to counter any respective weakness of the horse, so in the case of a very excitable horse, the rider will try to convey calmness with a long and stress-free warm-up. A lazier type will be made attentive by a short and energetic warm-up. And, the overcareful jumper should jump several smaller jumps, whereas the less careful one will need fewer, but more difficult fences in order to gain his attention.

Meredith Michaels-Beerbaum preferred to "cold-start" her high-spirited mare Rochette (the mare had her basic training at Gut Bärbroich, my father's barn). After the warm-up, she used to dismount and keep the mare in a corner of the warm-up area. Rochette calmed down and Meredith did not mount again until immediately before entering the arena. In this way, she was able to win several international competitions.

[25] Hölzel, Petra and Wolfgang, *Learn to Ride Using Sports Psychology*, North Pomfret, VT: Trafalgar Square Publishing, 1996.

▲ *Rochette ridden by Meredith Michaels-Beerbaum during World Cup competition in Dortmund, Germany.*

Practice jumps in the warm-up area do not need to correspond to the requirements of the course. In any case, the horse's energy should not be depleted. Problems that have been neglected during daily training cannot be corrected at this point by jumping often and high in the warm-up—it only serves to waste power, concentration, and confidence.

Some riders try to master their own insecurity by jumping very high fences in the warm-up area. A report on the detrimental effects of this habit was given by Hermann Schridde about his preparations for the Olympic Games in Tokyo:

> *We drove to a grass plot about ten minutes from our stables and built a training course. Schock-emöhle jumped Dozent over quite impressive fences, and so did Jarasinski with Torro. Winkler (riding Cornelia) and I (on Ilona) only wanted to do some minor jumping.*
>
> *After four or five jumps, I could not resist jumping a solid parallel of Olympic dimensions. Ilona made an enormous jump, almost all too careful. I told myself that I had to jump this fence again in order to encourage the mare to stretch out, to "let go," and gain confidence. When horses jump too carefully and too meticulously, it may be a sign that a jump's dimension is close to their limit, so they are frightened and jump too high. When those "careful" horses are injured when jumping, they get scared and may stop. This is what happened with Ilona. She refused the second jump and I had to do what I had never done before: I used the crop and forced her over the jump. We fell out over this. Up to that moment, Ilona had been in super condition, but this incident made her too unreliable to continue to be on the team.*[26]

[26] Schridde, Hermann, *Mein Tokio-Bericht* (My Tokyo report), from *Reiten, Reiten, Reiten* (Riding, riding, riding) by Bruno Nelissen-Haken, Fassberg: August-Bruns-Verlag.

Chapter 4

Fortunately, Schridde was able to ride his reserve horse, Dozent, at the Games instead and won individual silver and team gold! But, the relationship with Ilona, until then so successful, had been wrecked and not even a sensitive rider like Schridde was able to repair the damage done.

High-quality horses often give more during a competition than their scope actually suggests. This willingness to give it all—and sometimes even more—should not be used up during warm-up.

Focus and Rhythm

Throughout the course, the horse's focus must be developed or maintained. This, of course, is a question of experience. "Green" horses feel alone and abandoned by their pals when they enter the ring. They whinny and sometimes their hearts thump so strongly the rider can feel the beat through his boots! With experienced horses, too, it is necessary to be certain they remain supple and controlled during competition.

An intelligent course design plans for the preservation of rhythm, even if distances vary greatly. In order to encourage a horse to maintain his focus, do not to ride too often "against the clock." Hot horses, in particular, do not tolerate being "ridden to win" every time. Concentration and composure are indispensable prerequisites for continuous top performances. This continuity

A wall is an impressive obstacle that horses usually respect. Careful and inexperienced horses rather refuse than knock down a brick. Here is Lorina after one year of training, ridden by the author. She later became an international success.

▶

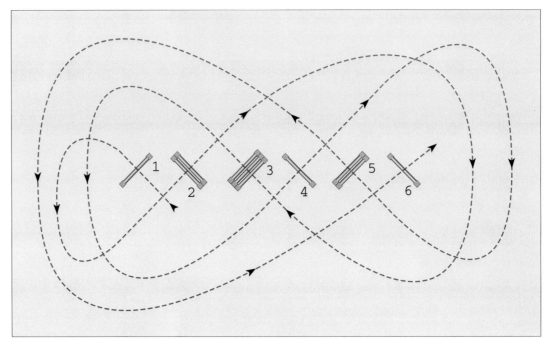

Training courses such as the one help to improve the young horse's rhythm and focus.
It also provides practice for changing leads over jumps.

does not mean that the horse's reserves should be exhausted at every course. A responsible rider does not ask a horse to give 100 percent more than a few times a year, even if the horse is experienced and at the height of his career.

To promote calmness and focus, it helps to deliberately take wider turns, for one thing. A horse should not be allowed to "rush into the turn" by himself. Taking wider turns also gives the rider the opportunity to improve the responsiveness to the aids between jumps.

Jumping a course should be followed by a phase of relaxation. Allow the horse to walk or trot for a while with his neck stretched until all muscles are relaxed, and his pulse and respiratory rates have calmed down so he can be taken back to the stable. The rider should do this himself, even though a groom could do the same. After all, the horse should not only associate stress and effort with his trainer, but calm and relaxation, as well.

Economical Use of Power

Young horses cannot be required to consistently use their carrying power throughout a whole round. It is, therefore, necessary to make economical use of the horse's power and only ask for that buoyant uphill canter that is best for developing an optimum jump during the turn toward the jump in question. Such tasks should then not involve stress, but instead give pleasure and develop a sporting spirit. This may mean a rider will need to choose not to compete if there is the risk of overexerting the horse. Experience is important, but steady development of a horse is not helped by frequent competitions with the sole goal of collecting as many ribbons as possible.

Jumping Against the Clock

In the United States, time is a factor beginning in five-year-old jumper classes. (In Germany, a horse may participate in competition "against the clock" once he is six years of age.) Introducing speed as an element is an enormous step, and it is wise to include preparation in daily training long before time becomes a factor in competition. The

In competitions against the clock, intense focus and steady nerves are essential—on the rider's as well as the horse's part! ▼

higher the speed, the higher the risk, too, and the more quickly and more precisely the aids must be realized and accepted.

Flatwork Preparation

Unless success is to remain thanks to luck only, responsiveness to the aids should now no longer be a serious problem. The balancing of the longitudinal and the transverse axes should be completed—for it is not only the shortening of the stride after a prolonged canter when "riding for time," or the short turn after a jump that require a willingness to collect immediately. The following principle applies: extension is the result of collection. The development of impulsion, straightness, and collection results in a horse that no longer tends to become disunited when asked to move at an increased pace.

Of course, there are horses that naturally have more problems with balance than others. This does not mean they are less talented—they just need more thorough training. Power Light, for example, was neither particularly smart nor rideable in his youth, and therefore not really fast when jumping a course. He needed years of constructive and solidifying work to be able to jump from top speed as he did to win the Grand Prix at Neumünster, Germany, in 1999.

During flatwork, continually increase and decrease speed. The intervals between extension and collection then become shorter and shorter while care is taken to maintain a consistent rhythm. Once restraining aids are accepted in a balanced manner, 6-meter voltes or flying changes should no longer be a problem when the first competition against the clock is tackled. In advanced work, a rather wide pirouette (a so-called "working" pirouette) can serve to vary and enrich the training.

The effectiveness of the flatwork can be evaluated by riding a simulated course where only the *lines* of a course against the clock are followed, without any of the jumps. Long, drawn-out curves can be mixed with short turns on the haunches, and prolonged stretches of canter are followed by a marked shortening of the stride.

Flying Changes of Lead

For the horse's first courses, it is sufficient to be able to land on the appropriate new lead (see "Straightness," p. 59) as the line design is made easy in the young horse divisions. Usually, a double change of lead is not required between two jumps. But, later in competition, a flying change of lead is indispensable. If the change is not executed safely and without hesitation, a disunited canter may result, which easily leads to a knockdown as the horse is unable to shorten his stride. Moreover, a well executed, fluent flying change saves valuable time when every tenth of a second counts. Therefore, it not only makes sense, but is absolutely essential, to be able to produce a flying change via light and inconspicuous aids at any time.

In a jumper, a flying change should be forward, flowing, and unspectacular; it is essential that the rhythm is not disturbed. Time should not be lost in an awkward change—the more easily flying changes are performed, the better concentration and focus are preserved. Compared with other faults, a flying change that is not quite on a straight line or lacks expressiveness is definitely a minor issue for a jumper.

When ridden by experienced riders, most young horses find it easy to change leads along with changing the rein. Some extremely balanced horses can change leads shortly after they are backed, even before they have learned other exercises. (In the case of a horse without the innate talent for flying changes, it is better to wait until exercises such as walk-canter-walk transitions and counter-canter are mastered.)

In flatwork, the flying change is often taught to young jumpers by riding across a ground pole, and as the horse jumps the pole, the rider is able to control the landing on the new rein (just as he does when jumping fences). The horse becomes familiar with the idea of the change of rein and his rider's aids, and will quickly realize what is being asked of him. Then, perform a change of rein across the diagonal or across the short diagonal without the support of a ground pole, and shortly before reaching the new track, flex the horse into the new direction simultaneously shifting your weight to the same side. Make it obvious that there is a change of lead to come. As soon as the new outside rein is clear, reposition your legs during the suspension phase of the canter (if the change is to be performed from the hollow to the stiff side, the outside leg should be used for driving). The new inside rein is yielded, thus allowing the new strike-off. When the flying change is safely executed, the leg aids can gradually be reduced until the rhythm of the canter is no longer affected.

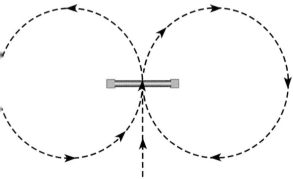

A figure-eight including a jump is not only for gymnastic purposes, it is also good preparation for jumping against the clock. Exercises such as this help develop the horse's instinct for going at high speed, and he will begin to think for himself, and in advance.

Jumping Preparation

Riding fast requires gymnastic preparation at the jump. By jumping a small crossrail within a canter volte or a figure-eight, the horse learns to either adjust to the new direction as early as still over the jump or immediately after the jump.

In speed competitions, a turn may then be begun during the jump. This is mainly achieved by weight and leg aids, as pulling one rein during the jump would only affect the balance and bascule of the horse. (If at all, the inside hand should only move sideways.) Even with an experienced horse, such a turn is not without risk. In the case of a spread, an early turn may easily result in the horse knocking down the top rail because of

▲ *The horse needs to be extremely responsive to the aids if a sharp turn is to be induced as early as above the jump (as shown here). If the horse resists the longitudinal bend for even one instant, a fault by the hind legs is inevitable.*

the shortened trajectory. But, if the turn is started at exactly the right moment, a lot of time can be saved.

■ Jumping at Angles

Prepare the horse for his new task by jump-

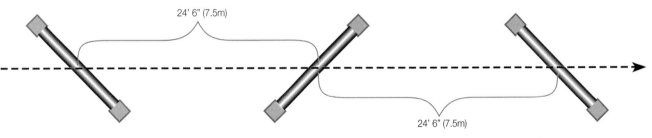

24' 6" (7.5m)

24' 6" (7.5m)

This exercise is a final test of jumping at an angle. In order to jump a triple combination such as this, the rider must keep his mount exactly on the ideal line. The slightest deviation to one side or the other would result in an incorrect distance.

▲ *The broadened trajectory is the result of a higher basic speed and an earlier takeoff. Much time can be spared in this way as long as the line is straight and a sharp turn does not have to be initiated after landing.*

▲ *The art of collecting a horse in front of a jump consists of controlling the forward motion by pushing the quarters closer to the center of gravity. In this way, the horse is compacted and does not lose either balance or impulsion or tense up in the process.*

ing from an increased—but rhythmic and relaxed—pace and by jumping at an angle. When approaching from an acute angle, outside leg and outside rein should be predominant enough to prevent the horse from running out. During training, if a single jump out of a combination is to be jumped at an angle, it should always be the last element. This will avoid the horse getting used to running out of combinations.

Jumping a triple combination built at angles (seen from a bird's eye view, p. 103) is a good test of straightness. The distances are measured from the exact middle of one obstacle to the middle of the next and should be absolutely correct. There should be no deviation from this ideal line. Once this task is completed without any difficulty, fences may be tackled at angles in a speed competition.

▆ Collecting the Horse in Front of the Jump

When the horse willingly performs distinct variations of speed during flatwork and

▲ *In front of each fence a decision must be made—and enacted—within fractions of a second. It is better to take a strong influence once, like this, rather than allow the horse to crash into a parallel; however, ideally this influence should not be directed against the motion, as this will cause the horse to raise his head, hollow his back and push his body toward the jump.*

shortens his stride after an extended canter without losing balance, you can train collection in front of a jump. Approach a small fence of about 2' 6" (80cm) from an increased speed. At first six strides—then four strides—in front of the jump, reduce the speed to such an extent that another stride can be inserted. You should achieve this, not merely by applying stronger rein aids, but by classical half-halts, which serve to maintain the horse's self-carriage. You shift your upper body further back and combine the regulating rein aids with driving leg aids. Each half-halt should always be followed by a short and inconspicuous yielding of the reins; the rider's influence should not act against the horse.

Jumping from High Speed

One of the first riders who resolutely trained his horses to jump from maximum speed was Hugo Simon. In innumerable jump-offs, it was his advantage to be able to canter a long distance toward a fence at full speed without any regulating rein aids. This did not

Hugo Simon was one of the first riders to include jumping at maximum speed in his training program. This is appropriate only at the end of a horse's schooling—and even then not frequently. Moreover, not every horse is suited to learn such an extreme way of going. ▶

only save canter strides—thanks to a longer trajectory, the pair used to lose less time at the jump itself.

In order to work on such a situation at home, two parallels may be built 131 feet (40m) apart (assuming the horse has a "medium gear" and the arena is at least 230 feet in length). Begin by covering the distance with ten or eleven canter strides at normal speed. Then, reduce the number of strides to a minimum of eight. For this to happen, the first element must be downright "attacked," and there is no time for a "wait and see" attitude within the distance to the second parallel, either. As soon as you land after the first jump, apply the driving aids again in order to lengthen the initial stride toward the next jump.

A horse needs a lot of focus and experience to be able to jump a higher fence "at full speed" without becoming flat or knocking down a rail with a hind leg. Therefore, jumping from high speed can only be considered the last stage of a long training scale. A young horse might easily become upset. Furthermore, this kind of training should not be performed frequently. This can adversely affect the horse's ability to read distances and his normal trajectory.

▮ Ride Fast and Conserve Nerve!

Riding fast is an important training stage but should not become an end in itself. For several reasons, my experience has shown that horses that are used in speed competitions often lose their jumping technique. The trajectory is cut short, not least because the horses come to expect a sharp turn after the jump. Also, if in the hunt for ribbons the horse's mental calmness and focus are affected, more is lost than won. Even when

"going for victory," the rider should save time by skillfully choosing short lines and applying his aids in the right dosage so that the horse does not come to realize he is going really fast.

My one-time trainee Sebastian Otten (riding Paloma) had become Vice Champion of the Rhineland and was qualified for the German Championship for Young Riders at Würselen. He had taken the mare over only a few weeks before from my brother, who had competed her very successfully internationally. She was an old acquaintance, as she had been bred and trained by me.

To briefly describe Paloma: she had always been very careful, and years of constructive training had given her a fighting spirit. She was top quality. On the other hand, she was not particularly "scopey" and could be touchy about the rein aids. When she was sharpened up, she either leaned on the bit or hid behind it. The Championship consisted of qualifying rounds that had to be jumped against the clock. The tactics were clear: ride fast, and conserve nerve! If the hunt for tenths of seconds disturbed Paloma mentally, her fighting spirit would likely be directed against her rider.

Preparation at home was focused on suppleness and lightness. As always, flatwork was aimed at keeping her hind legs engaged so that contact could be as light as possible. The final jump training consisted of a course at 4 feet (1.2m) including a small water ditch. The goal was for Paloma to feel comfortable but not overambitious.

Long lines between fences were meant to give Sebastian time to calmly re-establish self-carriage and balance. He was very successful: in front of every obstacle, he was able to become light with his hands without the mare becoming disunited. Both in front of, and after the jump she recollected and thus kept sufficient space between fences allowing her to perform a relaxed round. In order to wake her up 100 percent, we placed a "touching rail" in front of the last jump as a little "brain twister." She knocked it down, and we immediately took her back to the stable without trying again. Another go at it would have only served to "sharpen" her up too much.

During the Championships, we again met every morning for training purposes. We need to familiarize the mare to the atmosphere, and in addition, to activate her blood circulation. Flatwork was still aimed at honing responsiveness to the aids, but in her case, mainly focused on her inner suppleness. Diagonal aids were strengthened by longitudinal bending to ensure that Paloma would not back off the contact when the inside rein was strongly applied. Finally, she stretched her frame in all three gaits. During morning work (between the respective competitions against the clock), we jumped her a few times over a small crossrail to relax her.

The warm-ups followed the same routine. We avoided jumping high fences and took care to ensure that Paloma would not tense up. Again, work was focused on her inner and outer suppleness and the resulting concentration and focus. She rewarded us in her own way: by winning the gold medal!

The reward for riding fast and conserving nerve: Sebastian Otten and Paloma (great-granddaughter of Friedchen, see p. 12), winners of the German Championship for Young Riders. ▶

Trust and Obedience

A ny lasting and productive cooperation between horse and man can only be achieved through trust. This trust develops from quiet handling, kindness, and reward.

(Kindness) makes the horse confident, bringing about harmony with his rider in a way quite different from that reached by other energetic influences.

JAMES FILLIS
(1834–1913)

Harmony has to remain the goal of all training; it is the prerequisite for the acceptance of jumping by society—its ethical and moral justification. But, to rely on nothing but harmony during training would not get a rider very far. Harmony is what we all aim for, but this goal is only reached if it is based on trust and obedience. Athletes—horses as well as riders—can be strong characters, and these tend to clash, at least in the beginning of their relationship. The ability to overcome conflict, the search for compromise, and finding mutually tolerable solutions after clashes of interest, *these* are the touchstone of a solid partnership. No creature is like any other, and each has its faults and weaknesses (man as well as animal). So, what ultimately matters is the discovery of what each partner can live with and what must be changed.

One of the great dressage trainers of the 20th century, Otto Lörke, was asked why he did not want to record his vast knowledge in a book. His reply was, "I can describe in one sentence what training is all about: to further intelligence—to overcome resistance!" What did he mean by this? He was pointing out the narrow path along which horse training travels. On the one hand, the rider wants a confident, opinionated mount instead of a broken, subdued animal. Thinking ahead is a sign of intelligence and is therefore accepted, and even promoted by good trainers. On the other hand, this mixture of intelligence and self-confidence must be kept on the right track—the track determined by the rider. This requires a quick and energetic reaction to a situation and a sense of which counter-measure, and how much of it, should be applied.

Resistance

If we want to change the attitude of a horse in a specific situation, we first have to discover the real reason for the fault. A disobedience or a refusal to perform can be caused by very different reasons:

● Lack of experience (and therefore little confidence) on the part of the horse
● Lack of inner suppleness
● Excessive demands or an unfamiliar situation
● Bad experiences

- Wrong or weak rider influence (his aids not being accepted)
- Lack of discipline on the part of the horse
- Genetic lack of courage or willingness to perform

Trust and obedience in a jumper are two qualities that depend on each other. For the horse's talents to develop, it is essential not to wantonly destroy his fundamental trust in the rider and in jumping. This trust is practically innate with most horses. In the case of careful horses, it is important not only to preserve it during the years of training, but to develop it further. It is the only way to achieve top performance. Once this trust has been severely damaged (by repeatedly asking for unsuitable takeoff spots, for example) and has resulted in persistent disobedience, months of perfect riding are often needed until the horse is willing to cooperate again, and rarely will he develop into a reliable mount that is willing, if need be, to compensate for a rider's fault.

> One of the first horses I purchased, a mare, taught me the importance of developing a horse's trust in man before asking for obedience.
>
> She was nine when I bought her. She had generous lines, a lot of "type," refinement, and charisma. Her previous owner, a great stylist, had been at loggerheads with her. For years, he had been trying to jump her in varying levels of competition, but without much success. They were both hot-tempered and often clashed. Finally, it was decided to breed her, but she didn't take.
>
> When I first rode her, she reacted hysterically to even the slightest rein aid. In such a moment, she forgot herself to such an extent that she would blindly rush into anything in her path. There was only one option left to me: for six months, I rode her like a "passenger," on contact, but without flexion at the poll, and guided her only with weight and leg aids. I needed her to understand that I wanted to reach something *with* her—not *against* her.
>
> Then we participated in our first competition together. The mare would not permit any restraining aids or half-halts. As soon as I tried to shorten her stride, she had a fit. But, as she "came back" on her own well in front of the jump, I did not need to collect her, and thanks to her extremely good "transmission," it was not a problem to sometimes ride one stride less in a sequence of fences. With time, she seemed to realize more and more that I did not want to fight her, and after almost two years, I was able to work her quite normally and she won several advanced competitions, including the Grand Prix of Verden, Germany.

▲ *Cuba by Urioso A.N. out of Bizarre by Chromwell won numerous advanced competitions, including the Grand Prix of Verden, before she was sold to Italy.*

It is true that obedience implies basic trust. Occasionally, however, trust can also be increased by obedience. For example, when a horse is confronted with a new obstacle he is not too sure about, he might be encouraged to tackle it because he is obedient. If the obstacle is successfully jumped and the horse is lavishly praised and rewarded, trust is then increased. The horse has learned once again that his rider will not require anything impossible from him.

Praise as much as possible, punish immediately, but only as much as necessary: the punishment should correspond to the temperament of the horse. A slight rebuke at the right moment will often be enough to re-establish the obedience of the horse…When a horse does not obey, the reason generally is that he did not understand what the rider wanted or that he suffers from a physical defect.

FRANÇOIS ROBICHON DE LA GUÉRINIÈRE
(1668–1751)

Shying, Spooking

Among other reasons, resistance can be due to high spirits. It should, therefore, be understood among horse people that horses should be kept according to their natural requirements, which demand a lot of exercise. Only very rarely is disobedience an inborn trait in a horse; more often, it has a history. When a horse shies away from an object, "fighting" with him should be avoided. Instead, if he has not yet been loosened up, use another place in the arena for warming up. When the horse has become supple and obedient to the leg aids, he can then be

encouraged to diligently move forward (trot or canter) with a steady contact, and go on the bit. This active forward movement (deliberately produced by the rider) causes the horse to "pull" the rider with him (if the rider was "in front of the horse" in this situation, he would further resistance). The horse, flexed to the inside, can then be ridden past the frightening object on his outside.

Should a horse shy from an object and refuse to pass, then show him that there is nothing dangerous about it, especially not for such a brave horse like him. If this does not help, touch the frightening object yourself and lead him toward it with kindness.

XENOPHON
(ABOUT 430–354 B.C.)

However, if shying is due to a "spooky" character, the question—depending on the degree of the vice—is whether the horse is worth years of training. Nothing is more frustrating than to be let down after many years of schooling because the horse does not like some piece of decoration on a particular day. Sometimes, complete obedience may help to counter the problem, but it will not change the character of the horse and a trait that, at the very least, will always affect his suppleness.

My homebred Aperio is a horse that eventually lost his spookiness as a result of a routine and experience. During his first rounds of competition, he tensed all his muscles, his heart beat fast, then he turned round as quick as lightening and took flight!

I tackled the problem from two

directions: we drove to nearby riding arenas and show grounds to familiarize him with unknown places and situations, and I tried to confront him with only those tasks that I knew I would be able to make him do—against his will, if necessary. I wanted him to learn that he could trust me even when frightened. He had to be on the bit to such an extent that my determination won over his doubts about the unknown surroundings. Had he been allowed to have his own way, he would have resisted harder and more often. In this way, basic obedience was acquired by consistent and often stern work. But, when we overcame a problem, I praised and rewarded him, which served to strengthen Aperio's trust in me.

Early on, I had to put him on "high alert" in front of every fence in competition in order to ensure he'd remain "in front of my leg" and "pulling me with him," so I could override his hesitations and doubts. These first rides were marked by disagreement, and as he was not supple, he was not able to demonstrate his technique in the ring as he did in the warm-up area. However, he gradually surmounted his fears and was lavishly praised and rewarded. Maybe he thought, "It wasn't that bad after all!" and slowly gained self-confidence. Finally, he won his first competitions.

During the second season, everything became much easier, but he still needed an acclimatizing round to make him familiar with the show ground. He was taken over by my brother, but it wasn't until his third season that his stage fright disap-

peared. Only once did Alois meet again with Aperio's old problems. At Hachenburg, Germany, in 1999, the brass orchestra played as loudly as they could at the presentation ceremony. His muscles hardened, his eyes popped out, and even when he was back in his stall, his ears remained pointed toward the orchestra for hours. In the Grand Prix the next day, Aperio remembered the spectacle of the day before and when he had to pass the spot after the third jump where the orchestra had played, he suddenly shied the other side of the ring, and Alois fell off.

In following competitions, no other such problems ever arose, and within half a year Aperio won the equivalent of $60,000.

Head Shaking

When a horse shakes his head, the first problems that come to mind are with the mouth and teeth. But, it is usually caused by the rider. In most cases, it is due to a rider who does not ride sufficiently "from back to front," meaning his rein aids are stronger than his weight and leg aids (see "Contact," p. 49), or his reactions with the reins are not quick enough. (A running martingale may prevent the horse from withdrawing from contact.)

Rearing

"Almost any bad behavior or vice demonstrated by a horse is as a result of the hindquarters having been activated either poorly, or too late, or not at all,"[27] remarked Kurt Albrecht, former director of the Spanish Riding School of Vienna. Disobedience is usually "announced" by the horse beforehand with slight resistance. This is the rider's chance: if he is able to see the warning in time and remedy the problem, he may avoid a "fight." If it is too late for this, Xenophon suggests, "It is, in principle, best never to approach a horse when you are in an angry mood; for anger is incalculable and does what you will be sorry for later on."[28]

For example, when a horse tends to resist and rear during collected work, consider pain as the reason for this disobedience. Or, maybe it is poor rider influence: in a turn, some horses feel "pinched" by the inside rein and do not accept bending. Horses become quickly aware if they can unnerve their riders by rearing and will use this bad behavior in order to ignore all rider aids. Obedience to the leg aids is the first thing that has to be established and the hindquarters have to be activated. The horse has to "pull forward" again—to want literally to "go into the bit." As soon as the horse accepts the driving aids, he will also be more willing to bend around the inside leg so that the turn can be performed by the leading outside rein combined with the supporting outside leg.

Balking

Balking can be a sign of the herd instinct coming into play. When a jumper does not want to go into the arena, the reason may be that he had a bad experience during a previous competition. Horses have different "tolerance levels"; the less good-natured ones do not forgive a rider's fault. Balking also can be provoked by having the horse stand and wait for a prolonged period of time in the warm-up area. Also, never leave the ring in a straight line immediately after finishing the round. Horses with a tendency to balk should be cantered past the exit in a relaxed way before they are allowed to leave the arena.

Successful learning begins when the horse receives feedback consistently, mostly in the form of praise, and hardly ever in the form of punishment. Horse and rider should not be afraid of failing, especially when something new or strenuous is required. A certain resistance due to misunderstanding should be tolerated and is no reason for punishment. Rather, a characteristic of horses should be understood: should the rider happen to blunder, he must not worry because the horse is a good-natured creature and able to forgive shortcomings and weaknesses.

---

[27] Albrecht, Kurt, *Ausbildungshilfen für Pferd und Reiter* (Training aids for horse and rider), BLV München, 1992.
[28] Mayer, Anton, *Das Reiterbuch* (The rider book), Wiesbaden: Rheinische Verlags Anstalt GmbH.

Running Out

Running out at a jump is typical behavior expected from young horses, but even more often caused by inexperienced riders, when the horse is either not straight or not held by the outside rein and the outside leg. Weak riders try to change direction by means of the inside rein. Thus, the horse takes a firm hold of the bit with his teeth and falls out onto the outside shoulder. If, despite an experienced rider and correct guidance a young horse runs out at a jump, the rider has usually underestimated the situation, and the horse was not yet sufficiently on the bit. The rider needs to improve obedience to the leg aids by leg-yielding or paying increased attention to straightness, and will make a point of "framing" the horse even more distinctively with his aids.

During training, rails can be leaned at angles against the jump standards to act as wings. As a rule, the horse runs out toward his outside shoulder (when cantering on the right lead he will try to run out to the left—especially when the exit is on the left, too). In this case, the jump should be approached from a left turn (if possible) in order to keep the left shoulder under control. A horse that succeeded once in running out to a certain side will, most likely, try to repeat it. The experienced rider will be prepared and get ready to prevent it when reapproaching the jump.

Refusing

Trust is based on the horse being confronted only with such tasks as he is able to successfully complete. If he is afraid of a specific fence, it makes sense to use the herd instinct and have a safe horse jump first and follow at a distance of two to three horse lengths. But, not every disobedience is due to anxiety and not every refusal is a sign of lack of trust. These are other reasons why a horse may refuse:

- Inexperience
- Irritation (due to the rider's aids, situation, surroundings, etc.)
- Excessive demands
- Frustration (bad experiences)
- Anxiety
- Pain

Inexperience or irritation is very forgivable and an experienced rider will not punish a horse. When a horse refuses because he feels he has been asked too much, the rider can restore trust by applying confident aids and setting appropriate tasks. If a horse refuses out of anxiety, this is either due to the factors mentioned above or he lacks courage by nature. If he really lacks courage for jumping, one should consider refraining from training him any further. It should not be your goal to make a horse do something he has no talent for, or does not give him any pleasure.

Disobedience may also be the result of bad riding. Therefore, as I mentioned earlier, young horses should be trained by experienced riders, and inexperienced riders should be schooled on willing and experienced horses.

> **One refusal is a thorn in the horse's heart—any subsequent refusal drives it in deeper!**

If the refusal was caused by the rider it is not necessary for him (if he is sure in his influence) to increase the aids when he approaches the jump again. With sensitive a horse, the rider may expect a certain insecurity after a refusal, but he should only increase his driving aids should the horse hesitate in the approach.

Frequent refusals in front of a combination may be attributed to serious mistakes made during training that destroyed the horse's trust. When a horse hesitates in a combination because of one of the first three reasons I mentioned, the rider often tries to solve the problem by increasing his speed. As a result, the horse—afraid of his own speed—shortens his stride all the more and loses impulsion. It is much better for the rider to keep the horse in front of his leg when approaching the first element, as well as during the whole combination. If the horse does not "fly" over the jump but tries to solve the task by jumping higher, applying the crop at the takeoff may be more efficient than using spurs.

When a horse behaves out of character and refuses frequently—in spite of being correctly ridden—you should consider whether or not he may be hurting from an injury or illness.

Punishment

A self-assured horse may test his rider's authority during training. If he is sound and not under excessive stress, the reason may be that he just lacks respect for the rider's aids. When the rider is convinced that the horse needs to be called to order, he should apply the principle, "Punish seldom—punish hard—punish quickly."

Of course, there are horses that feel punished even by a harsh voice, but often young and uneducated horses only understand a more basic "language." When watching a group of horses in the pasture, one is often surprised to see the "give and take": manners are quite rude but are accepted by all members of the herd. This is one of the reasons why it can be necessary to hold one's own with horses that have not yet accepted man as their leader.

A skilled rider can often anticipate disobedience and evade it. It makes no difference whether he prevents such high spirits by appropriate feeding and handling, longeing, solid flatwork preparations, or whether he thinks ahead at the jump, avoiding conflict with clear guidance and clever course design.

The better the rider, the less discipline he needs to apply.

Application of the Crop

There should be a definite, distinct relationship between behavior causing the need for correction, and the correction itself, and when the crop is applied the result should engender respect. Applying it ineffectually will only upset a self-confident horse and probably provoke resistance on his part. Bad behavior should be punished instantly, in a reflex-like manner, as there is better chance that the disobedient behavior will be noted as incorrect by the horse.

Take the reins in one hand, the crop in the other, and apply the crop on the side of the hindquarters where they are packed with muscles—not on the loins where soft tissue could be injured. Frequent "stoppers" always run out to the same side after a refusal. The crop should be applied on this side to efficiently counteract this evasion.

During punishment, the horse should not be restrained, but neither should he be allowed to run off. Forward motion is the true aim of the punishment: the horse should go, or jump, forward as a result of the driving aids. If the horse is punished and restrained at the same time, he will likely react by rearing. Of course, he shouldn't avoid the aids by bolting, but if the crop is

▲ *Some horses always run out to a certain side after a refusal. If punishment is justified, the crop should be applied on the side to which the horse tends to run out.*

applied in the right amount, quickly and briefly, he will not try to do this. One or two strong whacks at the right place and time will normally be sufficient—more than three is not horsemanlike.

Application of the crop is not limited to correcting serious disobedience. It may also be applied at the shoulder as a light aid in turns, and at the hindquarters to encourage a more determined takeoff and prevent a refusal or a foot down in a parallel bar. In the latter case, the crop should be applied at the

hindquarters instead of the shoulder because the aim is to drive the horse forward, not sideways.

For training, a dressage whip can be used. A short crop requires taking the reins in one hand, which makes steering more difficult. The positive body tension that provides the determination necessary to jump the fence can be produced more efficiently by means of a dressage whip than by spurs. Excessive use of leg or spurs often results in the horse "getting behind the bit"; he is no longer in front of the leg. The consequence is a refusal, which in turn requires a correction. With a long whip, the horse can be lightly touched on the hindquarters by just moving the wrist, and this is often enough to prevent him refusing. The result is the rider is able to reward instead of punish, which is invaluable! In competition, however, a long whip is not permitted.

Handling the Whip from the Ground

The same goals that can be achieved with a whip from the saddle can also be achieved from the ground. Just as a handler uses the whip in free jumping, the main aim is to encourage a hesitant horse to jump a frightening obstacle. Of course, good trainers try to avoid refusals from the start, which involves giving necessary support at the right moment. Sometimes during training, a refusal is anticipated even though the task is perfectly reasonable. It is then that an experienced handler of the whip can ensure a determined takeoff.

It is essential that a handler positioned at the side of the takeoff area avoids any movement until the horse's eye has passed him. Support should always be given from behind: using the whip too early or from the side would only "catch" the horse between the handler and the wall or side of the arena. A good handler can also assist in the correction of a rearing or balking horse. A single application of the whip should be enough (this is why a skilled handler is essential) as using the whip is probably the most severe aid and should, therefore, be seldom used, and only as a last resort.

I would like to end this section by quoting from an essay, the correction of difficult horses *(Die Korrektur schwieriger Pferde)* written by Hauptmann Grosskreutz in 1940:

I want to stress again: the noblest way of correcting a horse is good riding. Much praise, seldom spurs or whip, and above all much patience and self-discipline on the rider's part are the sole basis upon which the goal can be reached.

Poling ("Touching")

As long as jumping has existed, efforts have been made to influence and improve the jumping process. "Poling" or "touching"[29] means that you touch the horse's legs with a bamboo pole or light wood in order to make him more careful, which sounds harsh, but it has its place. A more thorough look reveals three different areas of improvement:

● Concentration
● Jumping technique
● Carefulness

There are different techniques of poling for working on these respective goals. But,

before these are explained in detail, a basic question has to be answered: why is the trainer trying to influence these areas? Is he addicted to winning? Is it "profit" that motivates him? Or, is he using this method for proper training and safe development of the horse? Could he perhaps be trying to develop his horse's full potential? Or, does he want to protect the horse from a fall at the water ditch, such as could be caused by poor jumping?

This question borders on ethical dimensions in the sense of Albert Schweitzer:

He (man) experiences the other life within his own. He thinks it good to preserve life, to support life, to further to its highest value all life that is capable of developing; he thinks it bad to destroy life, to harm life, to keep down such life that would be otherwise capable of developing. This is what we have to think about, the absolute basic moral principle.

Poling is an example of how an action can be used for good or for evil. This is the reason why it is so difficult to distinguish between right and wrong, as well-meaning as the rules may be.

Variety of Nature

"Why not only use those horses that are naturally careful?" is a question sometimes asked by outsiders when they hear about poling. It is true that a quality such as being careful is not innate in all horses to the same degree. Let us have a more detailed look at the variety of types among jumpers. Very careful horses that should usually only be ridden by experts will often increase their

[29] A term borrowed from groundwork with dressage horses ("touchieren") meaning to touch a horse's legs with either a whip or a light pole to enhance his movements. The German FN tried to replace the now negative term "rapping" or "poling" after several public scandals [see *Richtlinien für Reiten und Fahren (Advanced Techniques of Dressage)*, vol. 2, 12th edition, 1997 (pp. 187–189)].

effort without having even touched a rail—just because they found themselves in a difficult situation. They demand consistent good riding. Examples of this type are Ludger Beerbaum's very successful money winners Figaro's Boy and Rush On. They were both incredibly careful, but expected extreme empathy from their rider; the slightest rider's fault was rewarded with a refusal. They needed a thoughtful rider of almost machine-like precision (as Ludger is) in order to be able to bring their full potential to bear.

Other horses can, more than once, bash a telephone pole with their forelegs without as much as "batting an eyelid," though nobody who wants to win should convert this type of horse into a jumper! There are horses that have simply no talent and will never learn good jumping. Really careless horses will never—by whatever training methods—become careful for long.

Some horses do not reveal a lot of talent when young, but they are intelligent, take pleasure in learning, and have a competitive spirit. In the beginning, they are often underestimated, but can eventually develop into outstanding jumpers. Others do everything the right way naturally, and nevertheless, do not become good jumpers later on. What distinguishes a good jumper from an promising one is his fighting spirit—a willingness to learn from faults. Naturally talented horses may learn more easily, but the decisive factor is whether they are willing to overcome the problems that will invariably arise during training. I believe that it is not only people who have lived in the jumping world all their lives and ridden hundreds of different horses who know that horses with a fighting spirit love to be challenged.

From my experience, overly careful horses are as rare as "cold-blooded clods"! The majority of talented jumpers comes in between these two extremes and may be educated to a certain level of carefulness just as successfully as some lazy types of horses can be woken up to the rider's aids by thorough schooling in order to develop their full potential.

Then there are horses that can jump very skillfully and willingly, but do not respect the fences sufficiently until they have hit one really hard. They often make good teachers because they do not lose their enthusiasm for jumping even when they are made to take off from the wrong spot, resulting in a hard knock. They enable their riders to learn from their faults. Every experienced rider gratefully remembers at least one such horse that offered him the necessary carefulness when he began his jumping career.

Because these amateur horses are forced to figure out their strides for themselves, they develop a higher degree of attentiveness than they would ever show if ridden by an expert. If they always approached a fence from the perfect distance, they would become confident they wouldn't hit a fence really hard and painfully (lightly knocking down a rail does not seem to affect them much). After years of being ridden this way, many horses that were quite careful when young tend to give increasingly less respect to the height of the fence. Others have to be encouraged to have more focus at the jump so the rider does not have to apply such strong aids. The horse should join the rider in thinking ahead in order to present a harmonious picture.

What are the means a rider can use in order to increase concentration, carefulness, or technique in his horse? Now and then, a rider is seen who—out of sheer frustration—applies his spurs strongly or shouts furiously to make his horse understand that he did something wrong. But, no horse will associate *this* kind of punishment with a knock-down, and communication between horse and rider simply drifts apart. There are other methods, which the horse is better able to understand if they are expertly applied. For example, if a young horse tries to avoid knocking down a rail by "dropping" one leg straight down in the jump, it is a potentially dangerous situation that can be remedied by skilled poling. The horse learns to tuck up his foreleg quickly and this prevents stumbling or a nasty fall. In this way, then, poling may be an absolutely legitimate auxiliary aid for training, much like a bit, whip, or spurs.

Between Taboo and Prohibition

Methods for making a horse more careful have been a difficult topic for decades. Much has been learned by "trial and error" and at the cost of the horse—and not every trainer was aware (still partly true today) of his responsibility to his four-legged partner. Originally, poling probably began by using massive rails: at the very moment when a horse took flight, one or two assistants lifted the top rail of a parallel or moved the back rail further away to make the fence wider—a rather crude and inaccurate method, and one that had the added disadvantage of causing the horse to hesitate and resist as soon as he noticed anybody standing near a fence.

In the seventies, Horst Stern tried to unmask jumping in general as cruelty to animals in his spectacular book *Bemerkungen über Pferde* (Observations about horses). Of course, the level of riding was much lower, but the author—himself then an amateur rider—underestimated the fact that top performances were, despite some crude handling, still based on the horse's cooperation and willingness to perform. Stern did not succeed in presenting the horse as a victim of man, but other heated discussions followed when scandals about prominent trainers and their methods of sales preparation surfaced. In the United States, manual poling during schooling has been prohibited for all horses

▲ *This picture, taken in a warm-up area during the fifties, shows that when poling is performed without any expertise, without skill and feeling, it has nothing whatsoever to do with training—on the contrary, the horse's mental as well as physical health is endangered. This horse was clearly asked to do too much. He had no chance to avoid knocking down the pole—placed too far after the fence—as attentive as he might have been. What is worse, if the horse had jumped only a little bit further to the left, he would have pierced himself on the stand to which the pole is fastened.*

competing in jumper classes at local or regular competitions. The German National Federation (FN) reacted by creating special rules in regard to poling: the popular term *barren* (what we know as "rapping") was replaced by *touchieren* ("touching"), from the French word *toucher*; certain techniques were prohibited outright; and those trainers who were actually allowed to engage in the method was limited (see footnote, p. 116).

■ Manual Poling from the Ground

The most versatile of these techniques consists of an experienced assistant lifting a thin "touching pole" or "rod" to improve any one of the three focal areas: concentration, technique, or carefulness. Moreover, expertly applied poling does not by any means affect the horse's willingness to perform. As with all methods and techniques, however, not only does there need to be an expert in the saddle, but ground personnel should also be schooled and skilled. If poling is applied at the wrong moment, with the wrong handling, or on the wrong horse, training could be set back for months.

Poling is best performed in the following way: a small and rather unspectacular fence of about 2' 6" (80cm) in height with broad, solid jump standards is approached at medium speed and at the perfect distance. The rider should frame the horse with his aids, holding him between his hands and legs without diverting the attention of the horse from the jump by taking too strong or aggressive an influence. The ground handler is positioned behind one of the standards out of the horse's sight, and from the height of the top fence rail, he lifts a touching rod (see p. 120 for recommended dimensions) so that it just touches the coronet band of whichever leg should be tucked up more over the fence. The horse will better understand the exercise when the rod moves with his motion rather than bumping his leg in the opposite direction. A hard bump, especially at the beginning of such training, would only frighten the horse and make him tense.

The hind legs should be poled first because this generates a certain forward pull in the jumping process. Only then are the forelegs corrected. Starting with the forelegs could easily result in a "delayed" jumping process.

In order to test if the horse learned from the poling exercise, another small fence should be jumped. It will show whether the two pairs of legs—fore and hind—are now evenly tucked up, whether the horse now focuses on the jump, and in particular, whether he transfers what he has just learned to another jump. If not, the process should be repeated, and the position of the ground man changed frequently.

It is essential that during this exercise the atmosphere remains calm and relaxed. If the horse becomes frantic and rushes, not only the leg correction, but *all* training is jeopardized. This technique is appropriate as a support to the rider's influence and aids, but it should never be used as a replacement for solid training.

■ The Fixed Rod

When improved concentration, a quicker push off the ground, or collection at the moment of takeoff is the aim, a touching rod may be fixed 6"–2' 6" (20–80cm) in front of the highest fence rail by means of a special rack (see photos, p. 121). The fixed rod is often used in combinations when the

◄ *The ground handler responsible for skillfully manipulating the pole should be as invisible as possible so the horse is not distracted by him and is able to fully focus on his leg technique. Ideally, only the front region of the fetlock or the coronet band should be touched. As with any other technique, a calm atmosphere is essential.*

horse does not collect himself sufficiently. The next time the rider approaches the fence, he will be better able to collect as the horse remains more balanced. It may also be hung after a fence if the horse tends to stretch out his forelegs too early for landing.

The method of the fixed rod does not suit every horse and, if applied without thought, may quickly result in a delayed jumping process, with the horse no longer "pulling" over the jump, and a loss of impulsion and buoyancy. It is particularly important not to choose too close a takeoff distance. The horse should always have a true chance of jumping a fence without faults.

This fixed rod is unsuitable for horses that are still unsure of their forelegs and occasionally "leave" a leg, as well as those that lose impulsion at takeoff and tend to delay the jump. The same applies if a horse is so nervous that he will jump frantically and heedlessly. Such a fault can only be corrected by calm gymnastic work over small fences. A fixed rod would probably only increase the problem.

The learning effects of the fixed rod are pursued in a sometimes cruder form when a parallel is jumped from the wrong direction. The result is a false ground line, which makes it difficult for the horse to see his stride. Because of this optical illusion, the horse may touch the rod with his forearm (above the knee). If repeated frequently and with a too heavy rod, this can lead to swelling at the knee. However, a *light* rod (see recommended dimensions below) fixed in front of the fence can be used without concern.

In the United States, touching rods made from bamboo should be a maximum of 1"/10'/4.5lbs (2–3cm/3m/2kg) and wrapped with adhesive tape because the or later affect his basic trust in his rider. Even the most good-natured and courageous of horses will, at some time or other, respond to this kind of riding by refusing. The same applies when a rider repeatedly and intentionally presents his horse a takeoff point that is *so* wrong the horse cannot avoid making a mistake. Experienced riders sometimes do provoke a fault in order to involve themselves in the jumping process, but they always try to remain fair.

In order to test or encourage the horse's carefulness without risking his trust in his rider, I recommend the rider determine a speed, takeoff point, and degree of rider assistance that are complicated enough to make the horse attentive, but still leave him with a real chance of jumping faultlessly. Making a horse more careful in this way—presenting a "challenge"—is absolutely legitimate and is a part of professional training sooner or later. This view was taken by Fritz Thiedemann, a post-war show jumping idol, who remarked, "Jumpers can only learn from faults." If the rider tries so hard to avoid every fault during training that the distance to the first rail becomes longer and longer, or if he goes so far as to apply rein aids at the moment of takeoff to try and avoid a fault, he will eventually have a negative effect on the horse's bascule and leg technique without getting down to the root of the problem.

■ Other Techniques

When a horse has become careless and needs to be admonished to be more careful, a thin wire is sometimes fastened to the jump standards at a height of up to 8 inches (20cm) above the highest rail. Touching the wire causes the horse to pay more attention.

▲ *Depending on its purpose, the touching rod can be fastened either in front of or after the fence. In front of the fence, it teaches the horse to collect himself and lift his feet off the ground more quickly; when it is placed after the fence, the horse learns to keep his feet tucked up better and for a longer time.*

material splinters easily. In Europe, bamboo of this strength and weight is not easy to come by, but wooden rods of hazelnut are of comparable value and do not splinter easily.

■ Getting the Stride Wrong

Every rider first learning to jump will unintentionally ride to the wrong takeoff point hundreds of times. Depending on the sensitivity of the horse, these occasions will sooner

This is used particularly with older jumpers that, because of years of experience, leave less and less room between themselves and the top fence rail. To a certain degree, leg technique can also be influenced in this way, for example, the wire can be fastened above the rear rail of a parallel if the horse tends to tuck up his forelegs unevenly or stretch them too early. A really careless jumper will not be helped by the wire, as touching it does not hurt, and if knocking down a regular rail has no effect on his jump, touching the wire will have even less. It is, however, one of the few methods of correcting a horse that does not jump wide enough over a flat ditch. This lack of care may have disastrous results, as should the horse step into the ditch, he may lose his balance altogether and fall.

■ Cruel Methods

Since money can be earned by jumping, there have always been cases of "blistering"—an illegal strategy where the coronet bands or the front of the cannon bones are rubbed with drugs that stimulate blood circulation, making the area momentarily sensitive when it hits the jump. Besides causing injury to the skin, blistering produces an unpleasant feeling that lasts for hours. Therefore, from ethical and moral points of view, blistering is not justifiable. Unfortunately, the history of jumping has known even more rigorous, brutal attempts to achieve a desired level of caution. On European show grounds some decades ago, thumbtacks, bike chains, and bottle caps were found under horses' bandages, and as recently as the Olympic Games in Atlanta, strips of wood bristling with nails were found fastened to jump rails. Such methods clearly fall within the realm of animal cruelty: they endanger the horse's health and suggest a deeply disturbed relationship between partners.

Everything in Moderation

Unlike the methods just described, some techniques for training concentration and improving the jumping process are harder to judge. Where are the limits? What is still justifiable? A solidly built vertical of 4 feet (1.2m) may be a trap for a young and inexperienced horse, whereas some experienced jumpers are able to jump a parallel of more than 5 feet (1.5m) from the wrong direction without losing their nerve. The method and measurements depend on:

- The talents of the horse
- His state of training
- The relationship between horse and rider
- The rider's skill
- The goal to be achieved
- The skills of the ground handler

When a horse has been asked for an increased level of attention, he may demand more precise riding from the rider. For the next round, he expects safe and correct guidance. If 100 percent of the horse's attention is required, then the same should apply to the rider. Generally speaking it is like this: when writing about a jumper's training, one cannot at the same time consider poor or incorrect influence from the rider. The prerequisite for the positive development of the horse is a rider who knows his business. Nothing is improved, but much is destroyed if in the course of poling or making a horse more careful the following happens:

- Suppleness is lost (the horse tenses up)
- Focus is lost (the horse becomes scattered)
- The horse approaches the jump disunited (he no longer "pulls through")
- Takeoff is delayed (impulsion is lost)
- The horse gets a negative attitude (he refuses)

The only remedy then is to return to the roots. You must build trust from the very beginning in tiny little steps. Therefore, I would like to warn you again:

- Never lie to your horse. You'll endanger his trust if you don't always give him a fair chance.
- Always keep the "working temperature" within the lower green range (see p. 47).
- Do not exaggerate your corrections; be content with small steps.

When in the course of time a horse becomes more and more negligent, the cause is not always to be found in carelessness due to routine or lack of talent. Lingering illnesses may affect the quality of jumping if the horse no longer takes pleasure in it and tries to spare himself by jumping with less power. The trainer should regard it as an alarm signal if he increasingly has a feeling of the horse needing a little "push."

There is actually only one thing needed in order to avoid the risks and traps of the tricks used to make a horse more careful: horsemanship. Horsemanship implies the ability to put yourself in the place of the horse when assessing a quality, feeling, or experience.

Fence and Course Design

Course design is constantly changing. It always has been—since the beginning of jumping—and still is a product of its time. About a hundred years ago, it reflected the pioneer spirit of the first generation of jumping riders. There seemed to be no limit to creativity.

▲ *Frankfurt, Germany, 1914. This wall was based on the image of the walls fencing in English pastures. The judge in the background recorded the number of faults—however many pebbles were knocked down.*

Yesterday—Today—Tomorrow

Tables, benches, wire fences, ditches, walls, and banks were all jumped, and many other types of obstacles such as coffins were invented. Depending on the respective country, massive fences alternated with extremely light constructions.

Harald Momm, one of the best riders of his time, reported the different conditions during the thirties and forties:

As small as the differences may appear in the order of the international events, they are quite considerable in regard to schedules, course designs, and rules. The Nizza Horse Show, which for many years has been the first international event of the season, is a military competition—the length of the courses asks for a good canter, good lungs, and sound legs…The London Horse Show takes place in July in a glass-covered indoor arena in the very center of the city. The fences look like beautifully made toys. There are eight of them, always the same ones, only every day in a different order, sometimes without wings and so lightly built that a swishing tail can cause a fault. Here, only those horses that have been specially prepared are successful, those that are calm and composed and jump very carefully…The Dublin Horse Show is a meeting point for horse people from all over the world…The construction of the show ground and the judging appear somewhat strange at the beginning. The fences are borrowed from the civilian hunting world and faults are judged according to the importance they would have in the field. Fractions of faults are calculated on account of

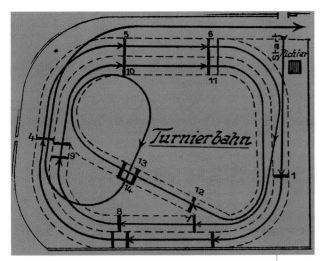

▲ *The lines of the first Grand Prix course in Aachen, Germany, 1925 rather resembled a race track. Despite the big loop at the end, there was no change of rein!*

And yet the courses designed e. g. by H.H. Brinkmann (one of the best riders of the Cavalry School of Hannover and later on one of the leading course designers) had such beautiful and seductive lines that for a rider with a feeling for rhythm who had analyzed and recognized the problems of the respective course, everything went right—as long as his mount was capable of jumping small "weekend houses."[31]

faulty jumping up and down the different banks or by the wrong order of strides.[30]

"Faster—Higher—Wider"

In earlier times, the distances between fences were not calculated as today. They only became more precisely determined when, at the beginning of the fifties, it became increasingly popular to control the takeoff point. Both resulted in higher obstacle dimensions. Parallel to this development, post-war equestrian sport changed from a sport for officers and gentlemen riders to an activity of mass appeal.

Beginning in the 1950s, course design underwent a distinct process of change. Fence dimensions and distances increasingly asked for scope and became the main factor in judging.

Jasper Nissen who at that time was a breeding manager, trainer, and course designer also remarked:

The fences often were so solid, the rails so secured by deep jump cups, they were not easy to displace; so much filling material was used, the rails were so thick and heavy and frightening that the horses jumped as high as possible— as long as they had not crashed into one of them or just refused.

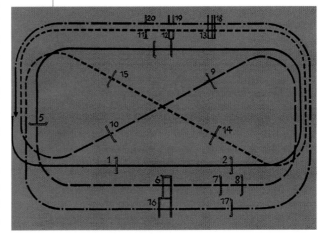

▲ *Olympic show jumping competition in Berlin, Germany, 1936. The course lines were still simple, but there were at least two changes of rein. Note: the triple combination had to be jumped from both directions.*

---

[30] Momm, Harald, *Der Offizier auf internationalen Turnieren* (The official for international tournaments) from *Das Deutsche Reiterbuch* (The German rider book), Rolf Roeingh, ed., Berlin: Deutscher Archiv-Verlag, 1940.
[31] Nissen, Jasper, *Parcours- und Hindernisbau* (Show jumping and the building of obstacles), Stuttgart: Franckh-Kosmos Verlags GmbH & Co., 1985.

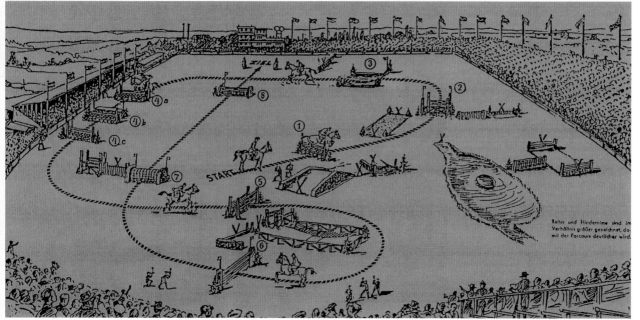

▲ *Finals of the World Championships in Aachen, Germany,1956. Half the obstacles were still so solidly built they resembled walls. Even careless horses hardly knocked down any of these impressive and easily assessable jumps. There were not any technical requirements, so participants had to be judged on the basis of refusals.*

This meant that in public opinion, show jumping was confronted more and more with the reproach that it was "cruel to animals."

More Compactness—More Technique—More Lightness

Whereas during the 1970s fences were impressively constructed with deep cups, thick and heavy rails, and on a massive basis, in the middle of the eighties the next change took place under the influence of Olaf Petersen. The obstacles were closer to each other, and the courses designed to be more compact. Furthermore, Petersen established light construction together with tricky combinations of difficult rows of fences. These technically demanding designs became his trademark. They tested the schooling of the horse and the tactical skill of the rider in a way that was, until then, unheard of. "With the same number of rails in a single triple built by Brinkmann, is nowadays built a whole course," some riders used to joke. Less filling material was used, the construction became more "airy," the rails shorter, thinner, and therefore lighter, and the cups considerably smaller and flatter. The fences were no longer bulky, which resulted in fewer falls and refusals, and increasingly, the order of the participants was determined by light knock-downs.

This development continues today. Present courses are becoming lighter and lighter in construction, but technically more demanding. Meanwhile, distances of eight strides and more are calculated. Different sequences of obstacles are placed in straight and bent lines. Since rails are knocked down more easily (on account of the safety cups, even the bars of a parallel are more easily displaced), horses are

◀ *A course at the beginning of the 1960s: slight knocks hardly ever caused faults. The fences were solidly built, the rails were up to 19' 6" (6m) in length (making for very wide fences) and frequently had a diameter of as much as 8" (20cm). The consequence was that the competition was not decided by knock-downs but mainly by refusals and falls.*
▼

required to be supple, responsive, and extremely careful. Riders must be capable of strategic thinking and applying an efficient, but sensitive influence. These courses are won by smart and careful horses that do not have to possess maximum scope: types such as Ferdl and Warwick Rex (Alwin Schockemöhle) were replaced in the winners' lists by horses like Libero H (Jos Lansink), Gaylord and

Figaro's Boy (Ludger Beerbaum), and Lady Weingart (Markus Beerbaum). Present-day show jumping presents a harmonious picture of riders and horses in rapid succession, thus fulfilling the demands of the media, which in turn complies with the wishes of sponsors, promoters, spectators, and professional riders.

Where Is Course Design Going?

In my opinion, current design development, too, is actually reaching a limit. The easier it becomes to knock down a rail, the more the group of horses that are naturally careful enough to fulfill the requirements of today's jumping courses is reduced. Why? We want a horse with a big stride, but also one that remains rideable. He should have a competitive spirit, but at the same time a pleasant temperament and character. He should have scope and boldness, but also be attentive and intelligent. And, because horses that combine all these almost contradictory characteristics are so rare, they are consequently very expensive. This, in turn, restricts the circle of those who are able to afford this sport. Jumping would be well advised to take its bearings and go back to its natural origins. This means that it should make allowance for a variety of talents and, if possible, offer a stage for all the different types of horses that take pleasure in jumping.

■ Offering More Variety in Competition

It is true that today there is a great number of different "Cups" and series offering competitive opportunities to those horses that do not really combine all the ideal characteristics but nevertheless possess special qualities. Why not develop a series of competition for horses that possess skill, scope, and boldness, but lack the ultimate carefulness? Where fences are solid commanding respect, and rails laid in "normal" cups? Perhaps courses could be jumped under floodlights as the contrast between light and shadow makes horses more attentive. Such a series of special competition could offer chances to a type of horse that has gone out of fashion, and young riders would be offered the opportunity of gaining experience over higher obstacles without having to be millionaires. The present level of riding and course design will prevent a revival of the old falls and punishment. In my opinion, show jumping would be well advised to offer a fair chance to as wide a range of horses as possible.

Change in Criticism

But, back to show jumping history: course design changed from solid to light construction. As I mentioned earlier, during the 1970s, Horst Stern had remarked that horses had to be forced to jump and, therefore, show jumping was equivalent to animal cruelty. This criticism has died down, and today, is focused instead on artificial aids and preparation and the attempt to make horses more careful.

The development of course design needs to be rethought again. If rails can be displaced by the swish of a tail so a horse is not even aware of having committed a fault, and if only abnormally careful or "specially prepared" horses are able to participate with some hope of success, then course design is taking a wrong turn. It is moving away from its outdoor origins and becoming an artificial product.

Alternative Selection Criteria

What could be the criteria for placement in competition if a revival of the old forceful methods is to be avoided? What could the alternatives be to knocking down a rail?

Today's course design—especially for indoor arenas and national competitions—has become rather simple. A course consists almost exclusively of verticals and parallels. At outdoor shows, ditches and banks are becoming increasingly rare. The obstacles are often presented just as advertising material and have nothing to do with objects found in the countryside. Does this mean more natural fences should be included again? Yes. It would be a good thing to have tougher tests of trust, obedience, and versatility. However, it would not work if by using frightening obstacles the number of refusals is increased. Any refusal disturbs the relationship between horse and rider. It would be interesting to watch a rider succeed in building up positive tension in front of certain difficult black fences but be able to relax in time for the next more normal jump. Another alternative would be to utilize show grounds with slight dips and elevation changes, which would put balance and responsiveness to the aids to the test.

At the national and international level, timekeeping is already a true means of selecting the winners, which is worth using more at the lower levels, as well. Time faults do not hurt the horses and serve to educate the riders to canter fluidly, without too much restraint and regulation. But, it certainly would not make sense to further tighten this means of judging in international events and convert every Grand Prix into a speed competition. This would be a mental and physical strain on the horses, which would

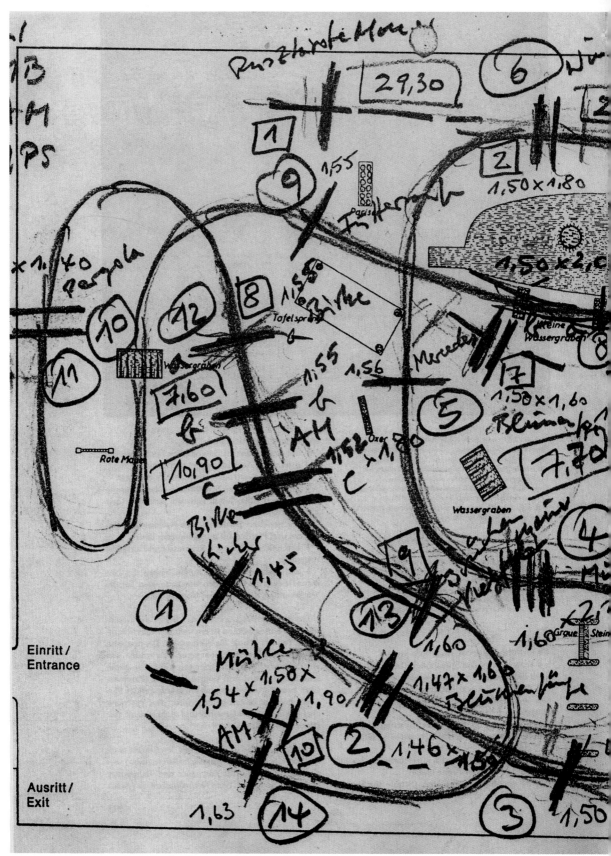

Another document of the times: the course sketch of the 1996 Aachen Grand Prix. Ideally the course design ref

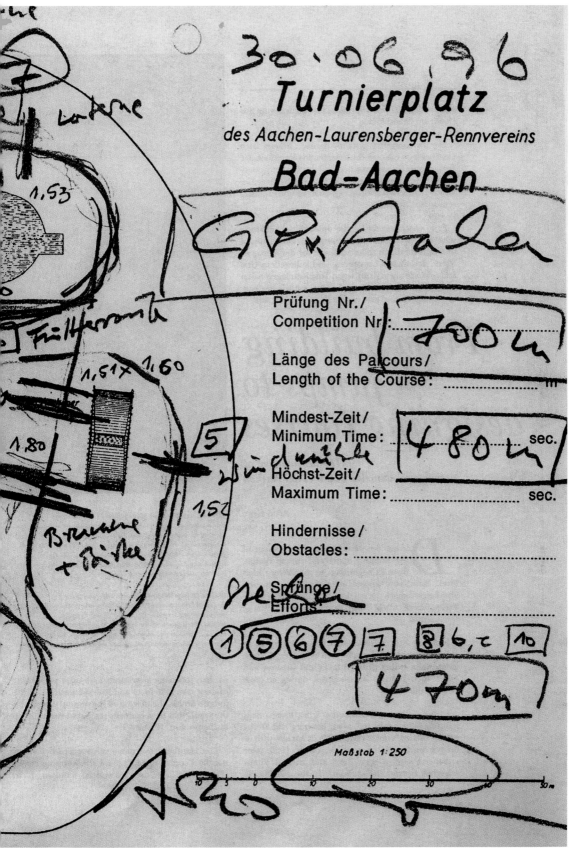

30.06.96

Turnierplatz
des Aachen-Laurensberger-Rennvereins

Bad-Aachen

GP. Aachen

Prüfung Nr./
Competition Nr:

Länge des Parcours/
Length of the Course:

Mindest-Zeit/
Minimum Time:

Höchst-Zeit/
Maximum Time: .... sec.

Hindernisse /
Obstacles:

Sprünge /
Efforts:

Maßstab 1:250

current state of jumping's development. What will future designs look like? Where is jumping headed?

be counterproductive to their continuing development (see "Jumping Against the Clock," p. 101).

Compact course designs demand more power than stamina. Would a solution be to intersperse tight sequences of fences with longer stretches of canter? From a purely sporting point of view, it would be interesting to see how horse and rider would "bridge" this empty space. The downside might be that this alternative would not suit the media. On television, rapid change of jumps, riders, and horses gives a dynamic impression, whereas prolonged stretches of cantering could be boring for spectators.

Whatever direction development takes, jumping as a competitive sport will continue to change. The fashion for light construction of fences cannot be continued any further without lasting negative effects on the sport. There is the risk of it becoming detached from its roots.

If jumping loses its connection to nature, it puts its right to exist at risk.

And, would it not be a shame if jumping—which combines dynamics, aesthetics, and nature in such a unique way—declined into nothing but a fashionable and trendy discipline? Especially when it had every chance of remaining a unique sport—of becoming classic.

Course Design for Training Purposes

In order to prepare a jumper for competition, training should be orientated around the types of courses the rider is planning to ride with this specific horse. He should choose corresponding fence material and suitable construction. There is another aspect to this: by careful selection of material and skillful course design, it is possible to avoid bad experiences, or even injury. The most important rules for a fair and appropriate course are as follows:

- A good training course should not contain any stumbling-block or trap, but, despite gradually increasing degrees of difficulty, be fairly constructed and test the strategic skill of the rider as well as the schooling of the horse. The art consists in presenting various problems that nevertheless can be solved with elegance and lightness.

- Wing standards provide optical orientation for the young horse and prevent him from running out.

- Less experienced or extremely careful horses can be supported in finding their stride and meeting the proper takeoff point by putting the basic elements of the obstacle and the ground lines a bit further in front of the jump. In this way confident and flowing jumping is promoted.

- Jump standards and cups should not have any sharp edges. Never leave empty cups hanging above the top rails of a fence! This negligence can result in bruises and cuts.

- To avoid falls when jumping parallels, cups should not be too deep (a maximum of one-third of the rail's diameter) and should easily disengage. If safety cups are not available, the back

▲ *Here, the chosen takeoff point is close to the fence. The horse should learn to collect himself in front of the jump and convert his trajectory from a semicircle to a steep semi-oval shape. A ground line helps the horse see his stride. In addition, a construction with not much air between rails, and a ground line further away, and standards acting as wings serve to make the task easier for the horse.*

rail can be placed on the rear edges of its jump cups. Front rails are normally knocked down in a horizontal movement, but the back ones are struck in a downward motion. As conventional cups and rails do not come down, this kind of fault can be very painful.

● The jump standards should be equipped with broad and heavy bases in order to keep their center of gravity low. If a horse strikes a rail (especially a parallel bar) and the rail is not knocked out of the cups, instead sweeping away the whole jump standard, a nasty fall can result.

● For training purposes, there should be as little play as possible between the jump standard, jump cup, and the front rail. If it's too easy to dislodge the rails, a horse will not learn from his faults.

● The length of a rail should not exceed 11' 6" (3.5m). The shorter the rails, the lower the risk of a fall because a shorter rail rolls away more easily when it gets caught between the front legs. For the same reason, the weight of a rail should not exceed 35lb (16kg).[32]

● A varied course design using different fence materials and a change of lines engages the horse's interest. In time, training may gradually proceed from the simple lines to more demanding tasks.

[32] Gego, Arno, and Hauke Schmidt, *Parcours-Gestaltung* (Show jumping design), Warendorf: FN verlag (p. 25).

Preventive Health Care

Chapter 7

Using a little foresight can prevent damage to the horse's health when jumping a course—the rider should be as concerned about the first "overstrain" as the devil is of holy water! Once a horse has had a problem with spinous processes, tendons, ligaments, or other parts, these areas often remain weak points all his life. Often, lasting development of his potential is rendered impossible because of early injury.

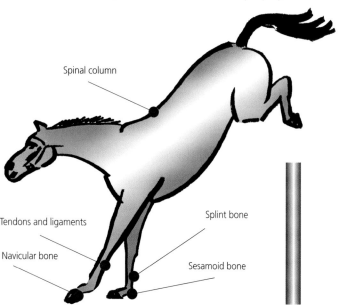

Spinal column

Tendons and ligaments

Navicular bone

Splint bone

Sesamoid bone

Expert training with gradual increasing demands improves the power of his endurance.[33] Nevertheless, the rider should always pay attention to the horse's health because aside from ethical responsibility and an obligation to protect animals against cruelty, the wellness of the horse is the basic prerequisite for his learning success.

Feet and Shoeing

The best method for keeping feet healthy is good shoeing and exercise.[34]

"No foot—no horse." Despite ergots and chestnuts, the hoof of the horse is more than an evolutionary relic of a toenail. In our professional veterinary literature, it is called *Zehen-End-Organ* (the "toe-ending organ"), whereby the term "organ" indicates that within the hoof, there is a pumping mechanism that is activated by the slightest movement.

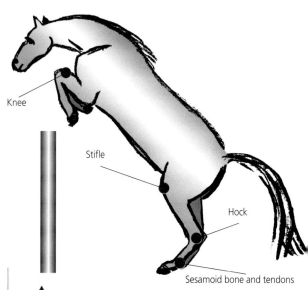

Knee

Stifle

Hock

Sesamoid bone and tendons

▲
This illustrates the jumper's weak points. How can injuries be avoided? The approach is complex: by considering endurance when selecting breeding stock and by raising young horses with ample exercise, the breeder may prevent potential damage. The trainer then needs to expertly organize the jumper's training regimen, continue to administer the best in care and management, and carefully plan the horse's first competitive starts.

---

[33] Huskamp, Dämmrich, Erbslöh, *Skelettreife und Trainigsbeginn bei Vollblutpferden* (Skeletal maturity and beginning training with full blood horses, München: Wak-Verlag, 1996.
[34] Bridges, *No Foot, No Horse*, London, 1752.

▲ *The dense and filigree-like clusters of blood vessels in the horse's hoof demonstrate the importance of the pumping mechanism for optimum blood circulation within the navicular area.*

Hoof Mechanism

When weighted down, the heels spread and the coronary band is drawn inward at the same time. This so-called "hoof mechanism" acts like a pump causing maximum blood circulation. There is hardly any motion in the lower half of the front wall. The slightest obstruction affects the blood supply to the navicular area, for one; therefore, experienced farriers always point out, "The best shoe is no shoe." It is interesting to know that when horses run barefoot with their frogs supporting their hooves, the consistency of the hooves is much more robust than that of shod horses. The heels are in a funnel shape, giving the frog more room, and enabling it to support the hoof mechanism. From this point of view, there is more to the care of the frog than just cosmetics. During motion, a strong, healthy, well shaped frog kneads the inside of the hoof and promotes blood circulation, which in turn is the best prevention against injury to tendons, joints, and the navicular system.

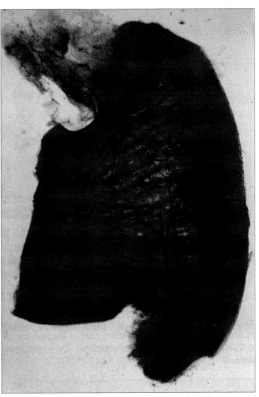

▲ *The navicular blood vessels.*

Unless the hoof horn is excessively worn off or ground conditions demand it, horses should be left barefoot as long as possible. It is better for young horses to make their competitive debut on sandy ground as sensitive horses tend to feel somewhat uneasy when first jumping on grass, and sandy ground with a good substructure is generally of such non-skid quality that shoeing is not necessary. The horse has enough to do getting used to the unfamiliar atmosphere of the show; there is no need to burden him at the same time with slippery footing.

Horseshoes have another disadvantage: in order to facilitate the action of the hoof mechanism in spite of shoeing, the horseshoe is nailed only to the front half of the hoof. When the heels stretch and contract, the hoof's bearing surfaces are worn off by the shoe and can be seen as "grooves." The toe, however, continues to grow, which after some weeks, results in a broken-back hoof/pastern axis.[35] The consequence is that the tendons and navicular system become strained, which is why it is essential to reshoe the horse at regular short intervals.

Shoeing

During takeoff and landing, the jumper is subjected to special stresses. The actual weight of the horse is multiplied many times over by the law of gravity. Good shoeing may reduce the risks; bad shoeing may increase them.

■ Landing

There is slightly more pressure on the branches of the front shoe than on the toe during landing. If in addition the branches are too short, they sink deeper into the ground than the toe because the pressure is distributed onto a smaller area. The navicular system and tendons are then subjected to increased pull. This means that deep or soft ground is an injury risk. These are the reasons why egg bar shoes (that are completely circular, see photo below, bottom left) are used increasingly for jumpers, although their advantages only just outweigh their disadvantages:

● When the foot is placed on the ground, hardly any "massaging effects" are sensed by the frog

A rolled toe on a horseshoe makes it easier for the horse to "breakover" his toe. ▼

[35] Launer, Miller, and Richter, *Krankheiten des Reitpferdes* (Diseases of the riding horse), Verlag Eugen Ulmer, 1990 (p. 43).

- They are pulled off more easily
- Centrifugal forces develop, especially at high speed, which result in tendon strain

Better distribution of pressure, which relieves the navicular circulatory system, makes longer branches on front shoes desirable. But, the chance of forging is increased when the branches are too long, and so is the likelihood of the front shoes being pulled off and jump-related falls as a result of forging during takeoff or landing. When a horse has a tendency to forge, the branches of the front shoes should be shortened (which, in turn, means shorter intervals between shoeing) and in addition, the hind shoes need to be fixed further back on the hoof. Forging may also be avoided by "rolling the toe" of the front hooves because the faster the front hoof rolls off the ground, the lesser the risk of it happening.

■ Rolling Motion

If the horse's toe has not been sufficiently rolled or the toe has grown too long, the "rolling motion" of the foot (the movement from heel to toe—the breakover) is made more difficult and the tendons and navicular system are overtaxed, which may endanger soundness. In order to enable the horse to roll over his toe more easily, sometimes shoes are laid further back on the hoof while the toe of the foot is rounded off by rasping to improve the breakover point.

With the hind legs, as well, toes that have grown too long, or heels that are too short, cause inappropriate strain, which may result in inflammation of the tendons or problems within the hock. The best means of avoiding these problems remain short shoeing intervals and long shoe

branches (which is not a problem behind because there is no risk of forging).

■ Vibration

A hard, non-resilient footing causes strain in a different way: it sets up vibrations within the hoof that older horses, in particular, find unpleasant. Pressure is distributed better and concussion is softened when horseshoe pads (leather or plastic linings packed with hemp or silicone between the shoe and hoof) are used, but they are mainly recommended for older jumpers that have to endure maximum strain. The demands made on young horses in training should not be of a level that necessitates this sort of shoeing.

> For all the high-tech products of hoof orthopedics, the classic broad horseshoe with long branches, short toe, and a noticeably rolled toe should always remain first choice.

■ Studs

In jumping competition, hundredth of seconds are often decisive, and when a horse slips, the approach to the next jump may be jeopardized. "Studs" are therefore used on more experienced horses. Stud length depends on the ground conditions: note that long studs on hard ground strain the joints in each turn because the hoof is not able to "glide" anymore. Long and/or sharp studs should only be screwed into the outside branches of the hind shoes in order to prevent serious injury to the coronet bands caused by interfering or by the forelegs being extremely tucked up. They should be removed immediately at the end of the round, on the one hand to avoid sores caused by the studs exerting upward pressure, and on the other to restore the correct position of the feet (a good horseshoe allows the horse put his foot down naturally balanced so there is no strain acting against the natural position of tendons and joints). Studs should not be used on totally unyielding surfaces, such as asphalt or pavement.

Faulty Conformation

Of course, the way a horse puts down his foot at its most natural and most balanced is always relative. A horse with flatly trimmed hooves may touch the ground with the whole shoe at the walk and hit heels first at the trot. There is no health risk connected with this. Horses that put the toe down first usually do not last long because the navicular system and tendons are strained at the walk and trot. The effect is equally disastrous if one shoe branch touches the ground before the other. In this case, the horse's joints are affected.

Many conformational faults of the feet can be remedied while horses are growing up. (If the feet are crooked, they have to be slightly shortened in the direction they are pointing.) But, during jump training we have to work with horses that have completed the major part of their physical development. If a conformational fault in a foot still exists, it must be accepted because at this point, the ideal conformation is the one that allows the foot to strike the ground in as balanced a manner as possible and without awkward action.

Prevention and Recognition of Lameness

The best way to prevent injury caused by overstrain is to respect the horse's natural tendencies with regard to movement. Free-ranging horses mainly move at the walk. Therefore, daily routine should start and end with an extensive period of walking. For one, this promotes inner calmness in the horse—he should not associate riding with the stress of learning only. For another, work at the walk serves to increase blood circulation and to loosen up the muscles. Some riders do not have time to do this so this task is transferred to a mechanical device or machines such as a hotwalker, which has the pleasant side effect of improving endurance since a machine can operate for a long time. There is, however, the risk of lamenesses not being noticed until too late if the person responsible for leading the horse to the hotwalker does not pay attention to the horse, or the machine itself is outside of his field of vision while he is busy doing chores.

Weak Points

When problems arise during training, such as horses lacking concentration or resisting the aids, some riders resort to tiring them out to decrease their resistance. As a matter of fact, learning is much more efficient when "the bucks are out" and the rider does not have to deal with the "oats" any longer. Some trainers make their horses jump every day in order to have them ready for competition or sale as a young horse, but this is not without risk:

Different phases of movement put the tendons of the leg under different strain

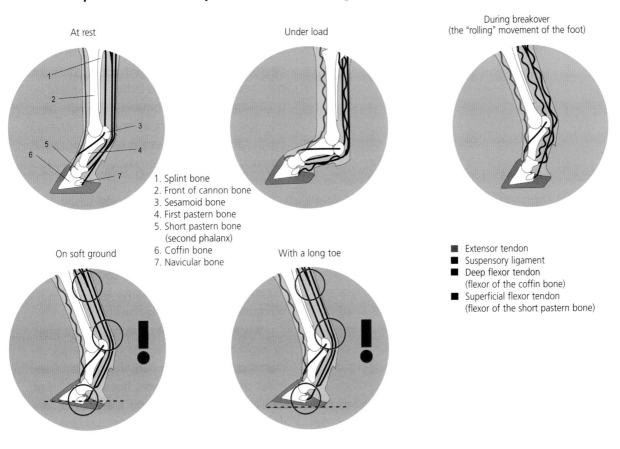

At rest

Under load

During breakover
(the "rolling" movement of the foot)

1. Splint bone
2. Front of cannon bone
3. Sesamoid bone
4. First pastern bone
5. Short pastern bone
   (second phalanx)
6. Coffin bone
7. Navicular bone

On soft ground

With a long toe

■ Extensor tendon
■ Suspensory ligament
■ Deep flexor tendon
   (flexor of the coffin bone)
■ Superficial flexor tendon
   (flexor of the short pastern bone)

Toes that have grown too long on account of poor hoof care combined with deep ground will overstrain tendons, ligaments, and bones. Enormous pull develops in the navicular system, as well.

When muscles get tired, they lose their shock-absorbing quality: all concussion is absorbed by the skeletal system and the ligaments. Especially jumping when muscles are tired, tendons, bones, ligaments, and joints are extremely stressed, which may result in diverse ailments and injuries.[36]

An experienced rider realizes from the way his horse lands after a jump when the muscles are tiring out. Or, he will avoid this moment altogether by allowing for extensive breaks and finishing work before reaching the horse's limits.

Overstrain is more frequently caused by rushing the training process rather than corrective measures. As an example: a five-year-old horse with the training of a six-year-old will, merely on account of his experience, be superior to the other horses of his age in competition. This makes the horse more valuable. Horsemanship is needed for a trainer not to give in to the commercial temptations associated with forcing training to increase the immediate

[36] Friedrich, Gabriele, *Die Erkrankungen des Sportpferdes* (The ailments of sport horses), Warendorf: FN-Verlag, 1986.

value of the horse. Quite a few potential top jumpers never reach their peak because of some weak area or other caused by "folly" in training or management.

Early Recognition

It is usually easy to recognize lameness, but in the daily working routine, other health matters are unfortunately often noticed rather late. Before, during, and after work the horse has to be closely examined. Does he have a duller appearance today than usual? Does he hollow his back when mounted? Does this joint feel a bit warmer than it did yesterday?

At the slightest suspicion of lameness or restricted movement, the horse should be observed at the trot (the gait at which a slight lameness is best detected) both on the straight and a circle, on hard and soft ground, and possibly uphill and downhill, as well. The horse should be as relaxed as possible so that a possible lameness is not obscured by excitement. The length of the stride is closely watched, with observers on the lookout for head-nodding or a one-sided sinking of the croup. The sound of the feet hitting asphalt or pavement can often indicate which foot is being lifted up earlier than the others in order to shift weight quickly to the opposite leg.

When the stride is not irregular but just shortened, it's generally the forelegs that are affected. By taking shorter steps and making a kind of rolling motion the horse tries to avoid the pain he feels when he rolls over his toes. He also avoids energetic forward steps because of pull on the navicular system connected with such a motion. Less impulsion and a shorter phase of suspension

also reduce the concussion and vibration he experiences when his foot hits the ground. He may stumble more frequently. If the hind legs lack impulsion and are not sufficiently engaged, the hock or the stifle may be affected. (Contrary to a lameness caused by a diseased stifle, a lameness caused by a bog spavin disappears after some exercise.) Hock and stifle lameness is often diagnosed when the lower leg is blocked with local anesthesia.

When the horse is observed under saddle, the reins should be loose and the rider should sit the trot in order to limit rider effect on the gait's rhythm. If lameness is confirmed—or even if some doubts remain—many diseases can be dealt with effectively by consulting the vet early.

It would exceed the purpose of this book to explain the whole range of potential ailments and injuries so only those conditions most often seen in sport horses, and that can be detected early by the trainer, are described here.

■ Navicular Disease

The skeleton of the horse is very similar to that of man. In the course of evolution, parts that were especially strained by the horse walking on his toes ossified: at the fetlock joint, the proximal sesamoid bones; and at the coffin joint, the navicular bone. The overlying deep digital flexor tendon and the navicular bursa together with the navicular bone make up what we call the navicular system. But, what exactly is navicular disease?[37]

In the early stages of the disease it is often the navicular bursa that is inflamed, sometimes in combination with an inflammation of the coffin joint. As the disease

---

[37] See Dr. Bodo Hertsch, ed., *Internationales Symposium Strahlbeinlahmheiten Dortmund 1993*, Warendorf: FNverlag.

progresses, the flexor tendon frays and the navicular bone becomes deformed. It is almost exclusively a front limb lameness (with one or both feet affected). Navicular disease is generally preceded by circulatory disturbance, which may be caused by straining, bruising, thromboses, faulty conformation of the foot, or contracted heels.

As shown by studies on the subject, a predisposition to navicular disease is transmitted by certain bloodlines. Small feet prevent good circulation. When hooves are short and steep, the frog is not sufficiently engaged, negatively affecting the pumping mechanism within the hoof. Other influences include management and climate:

● Faulty care during early development (poor mineralization of the bones or lack of exercise because of winter stabling)
● The horse's job (polo ponies, jumpers, and dressage horses)
● Lack of exercise (23 hours a day in a stall does not resemble appropriate natural living conditions)
● Dryness (the hoof is dried out by dry bedding)
● Poor shoeing (see "Feet and Shoeing," p. 134)

The disease may be instigated by other factors as well: inflammation of the navicular bursa (and possibly of the coffin joint) causes excess pressure, which in turn obstructs blood supply to the navicular system. Bruises and inflammation can also be the result of traumatic influences:

● Frequent sharp turns (especially after landing)
● Excess weight of horse or rider

● Continuous heavy strain without appropriate athletic training
● Frequent vibration within the foot because the horse treads toe-first or is often ridden on hard ground

But, the disease cannot always be explained. Again, it amounts to the factor of "endurance." There are horses who can bear almost any strain, others almost none. The trainer has a chance of detecting this insidious disease before it becomes clearly visible. First signs of alarm are:

● Reduced willingness to perform, less harmony during work
● Decline in basic quality of performance (making atypical mistakes)
● Changes in physical condition (reduced performance the day after strenuous work)
● Jumping with less power, landing at a short distance
● Slight stumbling after landing
● Short strides lacking impulsion

The vet has several means of verifying suspected navicular disease (hoof testers, flexion tests, local anesthetic "blocks," X rays, etc.). It is true, however, that in the past, X-ray findings have often been overvalued. It is more important for the vet and trainer to communicate on the subject in order to recognize this disease that is so often difficult to diagnose early.

Though common nowadays because of the way horses are kept and used, the problem has probably been known from the beginning of equine domestication. Vegetius (400 AD) described changes in the hoof which may be associated with navicular disease (Brauell, 1845). In the past twentieth century, navicular disease was often treated by "de-nerving" or "nerving" (cutting the particular nerves supplying the area of pain). Criticism cited ethical concerns regarding this "treatment" as it didn't cure the disease, it simply made it so the horse couldn't feel the related pain.

Today, de-nerving is seldom done. Modern treatment involves corrective shoeing and improving blood supply with drugs. Inflammatory processes are counteracted by anti-inflammatory remedies. Injecting hyaluronic acid (the thick lubricating fluid within a joint) or cortisone into the synovial spaces frequently involved in the disease has proven successful, and new treatments using calcium and hormones have been reported. When the disease is recognized early, causes eliminated, and treatment started at an early stage, the prognosis is much better than some years ago when it was considered incurable.

Tendons

The most vulnerable points of the tendon system in jumpers are the superficial flexor tendons and the suspensory ligaments. If recognized early and treated properly, an irritated tendon can be cured within a few days. If recognized too late, training may be interrupted for months or the horse may be rendered totally useless. Therefore, checking daily is the best preventive medicine.

Feel the tendons along the cannon bones for heat and swelling before and after work. Lift the legs and bend one after the other and feel again. This is the only way to detect any susceptibility to pressure. The superficial and the deep flexor tendon, as well as the suspensory ligament are then pressed between thumb and forefinger. It is not necessarily a sign of a pathological change if the horse winces once and pulls his foot away, but if this sort of reflex is shown every time pressure is applied, or if the region around the tendons feels warm, a thorough veterinary examination should clarify the situation.

Another warning signal for the rider is the formation of windpuffs, a bog spavin, or thoroughpins. Whereas thoroughpins develop from excess synovial fluid and may be an indication of conformational faults in the hind limbs resulting in overstrain, or of free-floating particles (bone chips) within the hock, windpuffs generally result from an inflammation of the tendon sheath. They are usually harmless, but their development should give rise to concern whether there could be anything wrong with the horse's training, shoeing, or the schooling ground conditions. When not conformational faults, these swellings are mainly caused by the following:

1. **Suspensory Ligament**
   - Unusually intense jumping for weeks or months
   - Deep, uneven ground

2. **Superficial Flexor Tendon**
   - Frequent cantering of long stretches at high speed (conditioning training)
   - Sticky ground (a recently ploughed field, for example) that "sucks" the feet in

Sesamoid Bone

The sesamoid bone is a small pyramid-shaped bone and belongs to the apparatus of the suspensory ligament. It is situated above the ergot. When the limb is under stress, this bone has to endure tremendous pull and, at the same time, is pressed against the surface of the fetlock joint. Blood supply is sparse in the area so their structure cannot be changed much by conditioning.

Sesamoiditis is a chronic degenerative disease of the sesamoid bone. It is a lingering and progressive process. Typically it begins with restricted gaits and shortened steps, developing into lameness that is intensified on hard ground. Generally, both forelimbs are affected simultaneously, one more than the other. Degenerative changes of the sesamoid system can be due to the following:

● Repeated stretching and bruising because of inappropriate training
● Long intervals between shoeing
● Faulty "corrective" shoeing with the heels trimmed too short

A fracture of the sesamoid bone is usually due to sudden stress exerted (landing/turning after jumping; uneven ground) combined with tired muscles. In jumpers, the forelegs are generally affected. The effect tired muscles have in exacerbating this injury can be learned from the fact that it occurs in foals that have tried to canter beside their mothers for a prolonged period of time.

The value of a sport horse that suffers from sesamoiditis is considerably reduced because the chances of recovery are rather poor. Therefore, I appeal to all trainers to nip this one in the bud!

■ Knee Joint
Swelling in the area of the knee indicates carpitis, also known as "popped" knee or

sore knee. It used to be called the "occupational disease of the jumper"[38] because it often developed when a careless or unresponsive horse approached a heavily built obstacle and found a bad distance, knocking down a rail with his forearms. Today jumping seldom causes carpitis. There are several reasons for this:

● Breeding improvement
● Advanced level of equitation
● Lighter materials and flat cups used for fences

A popped knee is not usually a serious injury, but in its acute stage may limit the mobility of the knee joint. If mobility is not affected, training can be safely continued but should be organized in such a way that any further contact between the forearm and a rail is avoided (being sure of the correct takeoff point, keeping fences low, and using knee pads, are examples).

■ Hock
The term "spavin" comprises any of several painful inflammatory diseases or conditions affecting the hock, including bog spavin and bone spavin. The hock joint is a very complex with several smaller joints between its many bones, the largest of which is responsible for the bending and stretching motion. The other joints underneath have shock-absorbing qualities. These smaller joints are the ones that usually suffer from any kind of a spavin. These pathological changes may affect cartilages, capsules, bones, or numerous ligaments. In the early stages, most horses suffering from a spavin will limber up after a few minutes, but later a slight or medium lameness may again become visible. If both

---

[38] Nissen, Jasper, *Springen und was dazu gehört* (Jumping and who it belongs to), Heidenheim: E. Hoffmann Verlag, 1968.

hocks are affected, it may be difficult for the trainer to notice the condition at all. It also occasionally happens that the typical ossification (fusing) processes of the lower parts of the hock do not cause any pain.

Safe methods of examination (other than the spavin flexion test) are by anesthetizing single, small parts of the hock, and/or X-ray examination. The findings may be diverse: decomposition of bones, fusing of the small bones of the hock, new bone growth, and cysts, are just some examples. Treatment depends on the type and scope of the condition, but can include corrective shoeing with thicker shoe branches ("raised" heels); liniments to stimulate blood supply on the inside of the hock; anti-inflammatory agents (such as cortisone) that can be injected into the joint; or surgery. By surgical means ossification of the lower parts of the joint is accelerated, severing nerves and sections of the tendon that run over the spavin and boring out parts of the diseased cartilage.

Prevention consists of:

● Correct shoeing encouraging the foot to be put down in a balanced, natural way
● Conditioning so that the system can adapt to the increased strain of its activities

And, for early recognition:

● Always watching how the horse moves, beginning with his first steps out of his stall

Stifle
Pain in the stifle may have many causes: bone chips, stretched ligaments, or inflam-

mation of the joint, for example.

When you lay a hand on the stifle while the horse moves, a shifting of the patella may be the first sign of stretched ligaments. Abnormal motion such as stringhalt or one hind leg striding forward less than the other may also indicate problems within the stifle. With jumpers, it is the inner part of the stifle that is most often affected. Causes may be:

● Abrupt turning motions (sharp, sudden turns)
● Excessive collected work
● Extreme strain by jumping often and high

On the flat, these horses have difficulty taking weight over on their hind legs, and in jumping training, too, a seemingly inexplicable decline in performance is noticed. The horse does not jump with as much power and energy as before. Horses that suffer from pain in their stifles tend to rear suddenly and apparently without reason, mainly in turns. The remedy is to call in the veterinarian as soon as possible and consider whether a more considerate working program (fewer fences, less collection, or even "rider-free" days) might solve the problem.

Back
As the center of motion, the back plays a pivotal role, not only for suppleness and responsiveness to the aids, but also soundness of the horse. The spinal "bridge" between forehand and hindquarters consists of vertebrae with different spinous processes that point in different directions: their fronts point backward, their posteriors point forward. They are all stacked between the cervical ligament and the strong abdominal musculature. When the horse

stretches his neck forward/downward, traction is applied through the neck muscles and the cervical ligament to the back; it is lifted and the spinous processes move apart. In addition, this motion is supported by a tightening of the abdominal muscles.

Back trouble is more common among horses that carry a rider, mainly dressage, jumping, eventing, and racehorses. Interestingly, many horses experience problems between the ages of six to nine. Younger horses may suffer, too, whereas those over the age of twelve seldom seem to have any trouble.[39] This phenomenon may be due to a certain selection taking place between the ages of six and nine: horses that lack endurance or exhibit symptoms of wear retire from performance sports. Stud stallions that are used both for show jumping competition and breeding are exposed to extreme stress because the strain to stifle and back is the same whether they are serving a mare or jumping a fence.

There are almost as many causes of back pain as there are symptoms. Muscles or the spinal chord may be affected. The spine may be sprained, strained, or bruised; the spinal processes may be deformed (kissing spine); or problems can be due to diseased limbs, resulting in disproportionate weight-bearing that may affect the spine when the problem exists over a prolonged period of time. A predisposition to kissing spine can be inherited, or the vertebrae can be impaired by faulty schooling. When combined with a tight neck, a tense gait may trigger the onset of the problem, as can jumping the horse until he is completely exhausted.

Unfortunately, damage caused by over-exertion often goes unnoticed for some time. As the authors Nowak and Tietje in their contribution to the *Handbuch Pferdekrankheiten* (Handbook of horse diseases) explain:

In specific cases, the cause is said to be a direct traumatic influence. In most cases it is impossible to find out the underlying reasons...If they are not due to trauma, changes in the spinal column can develop very slowly, over months or even years. The horse may not show any symptoms for a long time or may not show signs of disease at all thanks to suitable training that strengthens the musculature of the back. Most problems arise between the tenth thoracic and the fourth lumbar vertebrae. Tense muscles and sprained ligaments are frequently found in that part of the back where the front part of the saddle is positioned on the lumbar vertebrae.[40]

It is one of the trainers most basic responsibilities to assure tack fit, especially a well-fitting saddle. Back muscles and vertebrae should be felt regularly. Early recognition is the key: besides sensitivity to touch, there are other symptoms that should alert the rider to a possible ailment:

- Reluctance to be saddled or girthed
- "Sagging at the knees" when mounted, during a halt, or during collection
- Reduced action of the back, stiffness
- Resistance to backing or collected exercises
- Crooked or clamped tail, or tail carried horizontally
- Restricted gaits
- "Jerky" hindquarter movement at the canter

[39,40] Dietz, Olaf, and Bernhard Huskamp, eds., *Handbuch Pferdekrankheiten* (Handbook of horse diseases), Stuttgart: Ferdinand Enke Verlag, 1999.

- Standing like a "saw-horse" ("camped-out") after work

And, especially during jump training:

- Diminished jumping power or willingness to perform
- Groaning when landing
- Diminished bascule
- Clamped tail over or after the jump
- Rushing
- Half-halts before or after jumping ignored or responded to with tension
- First canter strides after jump with one ear pointing backward
- Difficulty navigating spreads

In the case of a serious problem with the vertebrae, prognosis is very unfavorable. (Once again, the first overstrain should be avoided at all costs!) But, it is not always easy to anticipate the limit of individual resistance to stress, as horses vary widely. Early recognition, especially of lingering disease, is the answer and constant attention vital, and there should be an ongoing dialogue between rider and vet. This is the only way to counteract possible ailments in time and prevent more serious damage.

Tooth Care

A regular check-up of gums and teeth is part of responsible horse care. The horse's specific way of chewing his food, or malformation of the teeth can cause sharp edges to form on the upper and lower molars, which result in reduced appetite, slow eating, or quidding (dropping) food. Before this stage is reached, the rider will often notice oversensitive reactions to the bit and/or heavy salivation. These sometimes razor-sharp edges have to be removed by rasping (floating).

Wolf teeth, an evolutionary relic of the first premolar, may also cause difficulty in the young horse. They are not present in all horses. At the age of four-and-a-half, they may push out, but they do not necessarily have to erupt; therefore they often go unnoticed and may be the cause of problems with bitting or contact. It makes sense to remove them as a preventive measure before first signs of oversensitivity in the mouth become apparent.

Chapter 8

Training
and
Ethics

Anything perfect does not stand by itself alone—it stands for a whole related world.

NOVALIS
(GERMAN POET, 1772–1801)

Ethics are concerned with questions of morality and a general primary responsibility of all human action. But, what is the moral dimension of horse training? In the introduction to *Ethische Grundsätze* (Ethic principles) published by the German FN as a reaction to a great "rapping" scandal, it says:

The limits of human action have to be questioned. To what degree is man allowed to use the horse for his purpose? Where is the borderline between the horse's natural physical and mental resistance to stress and overexertion? To what degree should economical reasons influence the use of the horse? How far may man ignore the horse's natural requirements? Should man be allowed to lose respect for the creature horse? None of these questions can be answered unequivocally. The individual experience, of the breeder, the caretaker, the pleasure rider, and the competitive rider are all different.

This sounds fairly dire. Is there really no common denominator among the multitude of groups concerned with horses? It is true that the doings of man are imperfect. Because we concentrate on a specific professional field, our view is focused as if by telephoto lens. Enormous progress has been made in the individual riding disciplines due to specialization and professionalization, but it has been at the expense of a "wide-angle perspective" comprising all disciplines. To say that no common answer is conceivable would mean complete surrender. On the contrary, in my opinion, these ethical questions can only have some chance of nearing the truth if an answer is found that is valid for all ranges of use without losing sight of the special requirements of the individual fields. This means that everyone—from whichever perspective he views the horse—should be willing to move toward the center. Just as a pleasure rider or breeder, a trainer should continually strive to justify his handling of the horse in a universally valid way.

As the man/horse relationship cannot be viewed by itself, another question comes to mind: is moral thinking, and above all, *doing,* a mere matter of character, or does man also need favorable hospitable conditions (a climate and a fertile soil) in order to develop such thinking and *doing*? History gives us proof: the more unfavorable (threatening to human existence) the circumstances, the less people are inclined to act according to ethical and moral principles such as Kant's imperative[41]. Unfortunately, food first—then morals is more likely to

---

[41] The German philospher Immanuel Kant (1724–1804) worded his "categorical imperative"—the concept central to his moral philosophy—as follows: "Act in such a way that you always treat humanity, whether in your own person or in the person of any other, never simply as a means, but always at the same time as an end."

occur when people fight for their lives, and "fighting for existence" seems to be found too often in the "horse trade." The threshold for the refusal or repression of ethical responsibility surely differs from one individual to the next. I would maintain that it is responsible thinking and acting that distinguishes man from animal—what makes us human.

I am life which wills to live in the midst of life which wills to live. As in my own will-to-live there is a longing for wider life and pleasure, with dread of annihilation and pain; so is it also in the will-to-live all around me, whether it can express itself before me or remains dumb. The will-to-live is everywhere present, even as in me. If I am a thinking being, I must regard life other than my own with equal reverence, for I shall know that it longs for fullness and development as deeply as I do myself. Therefore, I see that evil is what annihilates, hampers, or hinders life. And this holds true whether I regard it physically or spiritually. Goodness, by the same token, is the saving or helping of life, the enabling of whatever life I can to attain its highest development.

In me the will-to-live has come to know about other wills-to-live. There is in it a yearning to arrive at unity with itself, to become universal. I can do nothing but hold to the fact that the will-to-live in me manifests itself as will-to-live, which desires to become one with other will-to-live.

Ethics consist in my experiencing the compulsion to show to all will-to-live the same reverence as I do my own. A man is truly ethical only when he obeys the compulsion to help all life that he is able to assist, and shrinks from injuring anything that lives...

A commentary: reverence for life is a universal ethic. We do not say this because of its absolute nature, but because of the boundlessness of its domain. Ordinary ethics seeks to find limits within the sphere of human life and relationships. But, the absolute ethics of the will-to-live must reverence every form of life, regardless of its particular type. It says of no instance of life, "This has no value." It cannot make any such exceptions, for it is built upon reverence for life as such. It knows that the mystery of life is always too profound for us, and that its value is beyond our capacity to estimate. We happen to believe that man's life is more important than any other form of which we know. But we cannot prove any such comparison of value from what we know of the world's development. True, in practice we are forced to choose. At times we have to decide arbitrarily which forms of life, and even which particular individuals, we shall save, and which we shall destroy. But the principle of reverence for life is none the less universal.

ALBERT SCHWEITZER
(1875–1965)

This is what man understands as ethical action: bringing to fruition everything that is growing and opposing anything that threatens existence or progress. Thus, the human athlete takes upon himself effort and pain in order to develop his talent, and the rider additionally tries to develop the capabilities of his horse. This life-affirming, life-demanding, life-giving power—as manifested time and again in the rhythmical spectacle of nature—is implanted in the human soul. Call it divine light or love or whatever—it always remains the same. And, if it is threatened by hostile powers, it seems to come back (if it was not *completely* destroyed) strengthened by pain and suffering. Suffering may sensitize and broaden one's mind. It may awaken unthought-of strength.

This desire for progress applies both to the body and the mind. Ideally, everyone strives to become a better person, to reach a higher stage of development. In this struggle for self improvement, a person may often unwittingly cause harm. The gap between the aim and the result is caused, perhaps, by the many other factors that affect and are affected by any change of circumstances: family, the area where you live, the people of your country, and indeed the country itself. One could go further and say that every action has, in the end, a connection to every action all over the world, and even the universe.

Ideally, the dimensions and effects of human actions are, if possible, reflected up to their very last consequences by social commitment, protection of the environment, and the like. We should not only live by and from nature—we should live *with* nature, as well. It is akin to barbarism to utilize and exploit nature. In our society, fewer and fewer people get the opportunity of experiencing nature and feeling themselves embedded in it. And, where else than in equestrian sport is there a possibility of working on oneself and, at the same time, help the beauty of nature to develop?

At the Core: The Man / Horse Relationship

We come to the central relationship between man and horse whereby the practical reason for this partnership—the sport—is, for now, deliberately set aside. Difficult as it may be, jumping and competitive jumping can for once be considered separately. Anyone who has once felt what riding means knows:

Riding style is more than the sum of learned techniques and skills—it is always a reflection of the soul.

In his last great work, *Enzyklopädie der Pferderassen* (Encyclopedia of horse breeds), the equestrian expert Jasper Nissen describes the historical relationship between man and horse:

During the time that man and horse have walked together successfully, the horse has always faithfully reflected the changing attitudes, ways of life, manners, and traditions of mankind. In ancient times, the horse was closely connected to the gods. At first, he was game and sacrifice, then he served (domesticated) man: in harness, under saddle, and pulling the plough. Thus, a close connection existed between man and horse for thousands of years. It is hard to imagine the history of peoples without the horse. The horse has greatly influenced the ways of human living and had an important effect on the progress of history. Until modern times, the horse was of utmost importance in war. Invaluable, too, in peacetime, the horse was a means of transport and agricultural power.[42]

Today, the relationship of *Homo sapiens* to *Equus caballus* is mainly reserved for sporting and recreational activity.

Subject: Horse

For thousands of years, man has—by breeding and selection—adjusted genetic characteristics of the horse to suit his wishes and demands. Has horse, therefore, inherited the duty of serving man? Where is our justification for keeping, shaping, and using horses according to our ideas? Does the divine order, "Make the earth subject to you" give man the moral authority to exploit nature (including the horse) for his requirements? Or, have we got it wrong? Should we not create a more responsible "kingdom," be prepared to make sacrifices, and be a servant to its people? With this in mind, the man/horse relationship is perhaps a more symbiotic one, in the sense of the medieval, German nun, Hildegard von Bingen:

Every creature is connected to some other creature, every being is held by some other being.

HILDEGARD VON BINGEN
(1098–1179)

No newborn foal is born so "domesticated" that it wouldn't have at least, a theoretical chance of survival in the wild. Whenever (as a matter of fact, quite a few times in history) the horse was not a partner, he was made a servant, not by nature but by man. In former times, the horse has been used as a weapon, a toiling slave, a status symbol, and a money-making commodity. The latter two functions have survived, and others have been added: for some people the horse is a piece of sports equipment, for others, he serves to compensate for man's instinctive need to lavish care on something or someone. But, the relationship between man and horse always was, and still is, a reflection of society and its living conditions or, in other words, a slice of culture.

Some people argue that we would have to go to the zoo to see, feel, and smell a horse if he were not used for sports and pleasure. But, does this give us the right to see the horse as sports equipment and a status symbol? It is true: in the wild his life would be threatened, tougher, and more brutal. Nevertheless, don't we have a special responsibility for that creature that wholly depends on us?

"Listening" to the Horse

Doesn't this responsibility require us to try to put ourselves in the horse's place? To try to grasp his uniqueness?

Any successful trainer must have an intimate knowledge of his trainee. The rider, too, has to know his horse—with regard to his physical as well as his mental disposition. He should not only have a good knowledge of equine anatomy and have grasped the function of the individual muscles and joints, but he should also be a

---

[42] Nissen, Jasper, *Enzyklopädie der Pferderassen* (Encyclopedia of horse breeds), vol. 1, Stuttgart: Franckh-Kosmos Verlag, 1997 (p. 51).

psychologist in order to be able to imagine the feelings and reactions of his four-legged partner.

ALOIS PODHAJSKY, DIRECTOR OF THE
SPANISH RIDING SCHOOL OF VIENNA
FROM 1939–1965

From the specialized viewpoint of one who trains jumpers, it is like this: with expert training and a suitable rider, most horses (given that they are physically capable) are able to jump an easy to semi-difficult course. But some, even if they have shown a lot of promise at the age of three or four, are naturally limited. It is now a question of the trainer's ability to see reality; if he discovers the horse is not careful enough, not sufficiently bold, nor resistant to stress, he should not succumb to the temptation of trying to force more than nature has bestowed. This often is a hard step to take because it may mean admitting that an expensive investment is worthless and disappointing the owner.

It is not nature, but the ignorance of the rider that produces "rogues"; if the rider would study the natural capabilities of his horses, he would be better able to use them for the purpose to which they were born, and in consequence they would become good horses.

WILLIAM CAVENDISH, DUKE OF NEWCASTLE
(1592–1676)

On the other hand, some horses surprise their trainer in a pleasant way. Their self-confidence or their balance increases. They become more stabilized, mature, are more trusting and allow for precise riding, which compensates for their previous weaknesses. They exhibit a performance that, in the beginning, nobody had thought possible. The real class of a jumper often only shows up after thorough training and acceptance of his individual personality. If his disposition—a fighting spirit and willingness to perform—compensates for (or at least covers up) disadvantages, the chance of success exists. Helena Weinberg says:

> Of course, there is a type that is my favorite, but unfortunately I am not always in the position to select my horses, so I try to cope with what I have got. In this way, horses nobody expected much from suddenly come to the fore. One of these horses was Ferdinand—he was initially meant for the "small tour," but he grew with his tasks. Whenever the job demanded more of him, he grew a little more. And, all of a sudden, he participated in the World Championships in Rome. Nobody had known he had it in him.

The Hannoveraner, 7/76, August, 2002

A horse is only capable of top performances if he meets a rider who accepts him as he was born—who likes him, despite his faults and weaknesses. "They win in all shapes and sizes," a wise old saying from the English racing scene, is applicable to jumping as well. They are large and small, lazy and high-spirited, tense and relaxed, anxious and bold—all horses that have won important competitions. They all have one thing in common: a suitable rider who copes with their difficulties without trying to change their personalities.

Finding the right secret to every horse does not only apply to early training, but also to the training of experienced jumpers, as is demonstrated by the following story. When my brother Alois left home and went to work with a trainer (who on account of his previous successes in jumping had become a legend), he took his three best horses with him:

Sangria, a small, limited, but very careful daughter of Salut (together, they had won thirteen advanced competitions in one season).

Malta, a large, careful Holsteiner mare with lots of scope (among other successes, she had placed at the Eindhoven Derby and jumped over 7' 3" (2.25m) in Dortmund, Germany).

Frimella, a hot-blooded mare of enormous quality with whom Alois had his first successes in Nations Cups and gathered points in the World Cup ranking.

One year after going to the trainer, all three horses were doing very badly—they could not "jump" any more. They had consistently been asked for very short takeoffs, which robbed Sangria of what limited scope she possessed. Malta did not jump out of one-stride parallel-vertical combinations any longer (on account of the steep trajectory asked for at the first element, she landed on the forehand so the distance to the next element became too long). Frimella had completely lost her nerve, which had always been very delicate.

"Those horses have to go," said the legendary trainer, "They are not up to our standard." Alois himself was dismissed, "He is a really nice fellow, but unfortunately, not sufficiently talented."

So, Frimella was sold to Willi Melliger, who successfully jumped her at international shows like Calgary and Aachen, but unfortunately in speed competitions only. Sangria and Malta came back to us, and I was able to win several advanced competitions with them. Malta died shortly afterward from an injury in her stall, and Sangria was sold, and under her junior rider, participated in the European Championships and became champion of the Netherlands.

This example shows that a horse/rider combination alone is not enough; it takes the cooperation and all around goodwill of the entire team. It is all right to pursue a proven training system, but one should never forget to try to understand the unique qualities of every single horse—and every rider.

Wise Advice

If there is to be one generally valid guiding principle in horse training, it should be this one from a book on horse breeding: "Avoid extremes, keep the end in mind, and follow nature!" What does this mean?

Avoid Extremes

"Avoid extremes": this is easily said in our society where the motto "Faster—higher—wider" seems to have become the root of progress. Aren't we impressed when we see the impossible come true? When week after week horses jump a bit faster over the most difficult spreads, and when the turns become sharper? When the rider who knows how to motivate his horse to extraordinary performances throughout spring, summer, autumn, and winter is celebrated as "the greatest"?

"Avoid extremes" in a world that increasingly asks for specialization and produces fewer and fewer "universal geniuses." How many top riders only understand their own discipline and have but a fragmentary knowledge of the breeding or how their sports partner was raised?

The schooling and training of horses has always been subject to fashion and there are renewed attempts at exploring the limits. But, in my opinion, the ideas that have been considered valid for hundreds, even thousands, of years are far more valuable for a trainer than all the tricks, and "guru" methods, most importantly because they avoid "extremes," and have stood the test of time.

Keep the End in Mind

"Keep the end in mind": this does not necessarily mean the end of schooling or even the end of the horse's competitive career, but instead, a worthy parting of ways before a lifetime of injury and wear leaves nothing but permanent and painful infirmities, and before a once celebrated career ends up in smaller and smaller competitions until nothing goes right anymore. It could also mean a look back at one's own life, questioning: whether appearance and reality did not differ too widely; whether, in the end, the price for success was not too high; whether a fellow creature did not have to suffer from worship of the "golden calf."

It might even mean the end of a whole era in which top athletic performances were equated with social advancement and were, consequently, fought for at (almost) any cost. Basic human requirements such as seeking acceptance and developing one's potential are the mainsprings for any athlete, and thus of sports as a whole. Can you imagine a society in which this urge is no longer applauded? Should public opinion really matter so much when you consider the ethical and moral point of view? Can social acceptance offer true orientation to anybody who is looking for the right way of training—for the truth?

History shows that society can, at best, claim one of several points of view. Thus, the public's opinion of punishing an animal changed with time. After a war, the attitude toward misery, sorrow, and violence is different than in times of peace. Man and animal alike have to endure infinite suffering during wars and are affected by the fight for survival—and by the ascent out of ruin. My father was one of many who, with the help of working horses, risked their lives ploughing fields strewn with bombs in order to make them fertile again. In one field alone, he discovered more than thirty duds. He and his horses were lucky because none of the shells exploded, but the danger was always omnipresent.

In this post-war climate, Fritz Thiedemann became a national hero when he gained international reputation for Germany with "cart horses," which judging by today's standards, were more or less unsuitable for jumping. The motto was: "Make something out of nothing." There were no alternatives,

no options. Videos of his rides sometimes appear strange today—for example, when he won the Hamburg Derby in record time, he so mercilessly used his spurs that his mount, the gray mare Retina, was bleeding in front of and behind the girth. Gerd Wiltfang once remarked disparagingly, "That one rode with whip and spurs!" I do not want to detract in any way from his life's work; I feel the deepest respect for his versatile abilities as a rider as well as for his exemplary character unmatched even today. I am only demonstrating the changes of course public opinion can take over 50 years. Today, a rider who gives his horse a brief slap is bound to be booed by spectators, and in some circles, the act of riding itself is considered cruel.

Today, the danger actually is in animals being anthropomorphised: human wishes and emotions are transferred onto them, and in this artificial world, human understanding for the *real* requirements and feelings of animals is lost more and more.

If we consider the question of universal responsibility extending beyond our own deaths, we are involuntarily confronted with questions of faith. In this context, I want to share a strange encounter I had some time ago. In our small home town, I met my former French teacher, an odd character who even after twenty years appeared unchanged: a sturdy, neckless, bald man who, in a grotesque way, underlined his words with filigree movements of his broad, rough hands. He had an untidy look about him—he probably just did not care what he looked like. Of his teaching, I remember little French, but quite a few of his remarks about the

German campaign against Russia, which had been as cruel for men as it had been for horses.

I told him who I was, but at first he could not place me. A few key words such as my name and the name of our farm gave him a clue.

"Isn't someone from your family quite a successful rider?" he asked.

"Yes, my brother," I confirmed.

"What does he do, dressage or..." he paused and made a face as if he had bitten into a lemon, "...or jumping?"

"Jumping!" I replied.

"But isn't it cruel to horses?"

"No," I answered. "Perhaps it depends on the way it is done."

He remained obviously sceptical and put on a broad artificial grin as if he wanted to hide his real feelings.

"I don't know whether God will see it like that, too," he stated. "Well, it probably isn't so bad as in the war—people suffered, but it was their own fault. The horses, though—what did they have to do with it?"

At first I thought, how could he see any comparison or parallel at all? Maybe he was a belated victim of distorted media reports. But despite his thinking in clichés, I could not dismiss him because I was impressed by the level to which he raised our short conversation by means of this question, and I had to confess to myself that the subject of "primary responsibility" had concerned me for years.

In a thousand years, will jumping be regarded with the same uncomprehending disgust as when we look back now at the fights of the Roman gladiators? Will it be considered a product of the human obsession with acquiring status? Or perhaps a product of a leisure society obsessed with sport? Just because we have the power, do we really have the right to treat horses as sporting equipment, or as mere objects of prestige? Who or what could serve as the judge? Where do we find everlasting truth?

Aristotle said, "Truth is to be found in the very inside of things."

Follow Nature

People who understand the idea of "God" to comprise life and love, as well as love for life and for creation, will "follow nature." All our perceived "knowledge" about the horse can merely approximate to the truth, at best. The infinite diversity of nature is reflected in each individual, and therefore the trainer of jumping horses must be willing to do justice to the uniqueness of each horse. "Listening to the horse is what does it" is Ludger Beerbaum's[43] credo, too. The more jumping moves away from nature, the sooner it will lose its justification. To return to its roots could mean:

- To take into account the former steppe animal's requirements with regard to his management and work.
- Not to reduce a jumping course to a sequence of "advertisements," but to design it in such a way so as to emphasize its connection to the outdoors.
- Not to use jump cups that are so flat that a horse will not notice a knock-down so, therefore, cannot be expected to show a reaction (one way riders are pushed to

---

[43] Beerbaum, Ludger and Susanne Strübel, *Erfolg ist kein Zufall* (Success is not coincidence), Stuttgart: Kosmos Verlag, 1999.

manipulate carefulness, for example, by blistering).

- Not to regard a top jumper as a Formula One car equipped with small screws that can be fiddled about with until maximum performance is reached.
- To allow for times of healing and give ample rest, especially in high-performance sports.
- To allow for development, maturity, but also for ageing and breakdown; a true horseman will also permit the slow, gradual training and conditioning of his horses (not exactly a rider's dream). As is generally known, patience is very difficult when waiting for a real prodigy to develop.

This might be compared to a child with an outstanding talent for playing the violin. The child's path to perfection is partly dependent on teachers not cluttering his progress by commercializing his talent in "child-prodigy shows." The training of an elite jumper could also be compared to that of a singer who needs solid basic schooling

Our responsibility to any fellow creature is to determine whether pain is to be seen as an acceptable stimulus for improved performance or as destructive exploitation. ▼

and then years of patience until his voice has matured. Now and then he is confronted with a difficult score, which is then put aside again for months until the process of maturing is completed.

The goal cannot be for a jumper's career to peak when he is four or five years old. This may seem uneconomical to some horse owners when they add together all their expenses, but economy and ethics are not necessarily antagonistic. If the owner or breeder of a young horse is convinced of the horse's special capabilities, it may very well pay in the end to relinquish the "quick money" to ensure a long-term progressive training regimen.

Furthermore, a responsible rider will try to take into account the biological rhythm of the horses under his charge and not demand top performances throughout the year. If injuries occur despite all his care, he will give them time to heal; he will allow for regenerative phases after more strenuous work, even if this means that he has to miss one or more lucrative shows. "There is a serious danger of horses being overworked and competed too frequently because there is more money to gain. Pursuing a well-planned season is made harder for the riders,"[44] warned Dr. Reiner Klimke shortly before his death.

One of the main rules is that equitation should never be performed against nature. On the contrary, one should try to imitate nature and follow nature, even improve nature if it is possible.

GEORG ENGELHARD VON LÖHNEYSEN

(1552–1622)

Cultural Value and Equitation

In a unique way, jumping reflects the aesthetics and dynamics of nature. As man and nature drift further apart training jumpers is an affirming way to again feel the oneness with nature, the common roots of evolution, and also the respect for creation, thus enriching our own souls.

"It is true that today, most horses are managed better than before: we think much more about how to keep them according to their essential needs," Dr. Klimke pointed out in his last interview. "In my opinion, however, with many trainers, their basic attitude toward horses is wrong. 'I love my horse' is often said by young girls, but very rarely by a trainer."

Is this not an unusual thought when uttered by an ambitious Olympic winner and pragmatic lawyer? Within the circles in which Dr. Klimke (an exemplary and versatile rider) moved, this might sound like an emotional slip, but it really was a last all-embracing appeal to not become arrogant in the dominance of the horse and the control of his development. Not only should we respect our fellow creature, the horse, but moreover we should preserve the admiration and love that every one of us feels at the beginning of our equestrian careers—and despite all our professional approaches to training, not to lose the life-giving, life-promoting power of love. To love creation in the horse—this is, without doubt, the noblest goal.

---

[44] Van Leeuwen, J.B.F., *Das Pferd im 20. Jahrhundert—100 Jahre Pferdesport in 100 Interviews* (The horse in the 20th century: 100 years of horse sport in 100 interviews), Maarsen: Premium Press, 1999.

Page numbers in *italic* indicate photographs or illustrations.